Unseen Forces
Beyond This World

Unseen Forces
Beyond This World

by Phillip & Fern Halverson

Harrison House
Tulsa, Oklahoma

Unseen Forces Beyond This World
ISBN 1-57794-253-1
Copyright © 2000 by Fern Halverson
Living Word Christian Center
9201 75th Avenue North
Brooklyn Park, Minnesota 55428

Published by Harrison House, Inc.
P. O. Box 35035
Tulsa, Oklahoma 74153

Dedication

To

Vicki Jamison-Peterson,

with whom we first entered

into a vital ministry.

Vicki is gentle, patient, long-suffering and has the power to endure with a good temperament whatever comes. She has enfolded herself and those around her in forgiving love and harmony. (Col. 3:12-14.)

Contents

Foreword

My Beginnings
by Phillip Halverson

I encountered the dynamic moving of the Holy Spirit early in life. Born the second son of Norwegian parents, I did not speak or understand English until I began school at seven years of age.

Our Wisconsin farm life was hard and demanding with eight children to support. My father's forefathers homesteaded in Wisconsin and helped build the Lutheran churches in our predominantly Norwegian community, which was full of relatives from both sides of the family.

My mother, Inga, was saved and later journeyed by horse and buggy to Alexandria, Minnesota, with her sister, Tilda, where she received the mighty baptism in the Holy Spirit at the famous tent meetings of Maria Woodworth-Etter.

After she came back home from that meeting, I was conceived. I believe there was a transmittal of divine power through Sister Etter to me through my mother's fresh experience.

Edwin, my father, then gave his consent for prayer meetings to be held in our farm home, even though at that time he was not a born-again believer.

I was only six years old, not speaking or understanding English at all, when two Irish youths came with others to our home for an afternoon prayer meeting.

My father came in to fire up the woodstove, as usual, and was sitting with his favorite corncob pipe in his mouth and with me on his lap.

After tarrying for the Holy Spirit, which was common in those days, the two Irish boys suddenly walked over to my father and began speaking to him in perfect Norwegian—a language they had never learned!

They told him of God's great love, expounding on the faithfulness of the Lord and how God blesses those who serve Him. Jesus was magnified!

This supernatural encounter with the Holy Spirit transformed my father into a dedicated and faithful believer from that day forward, and it made a mark in my spirit.

Eye hath not seen, nor ear heard, neither have entered into the heart of man, the things which God hath prepared for them that love him.

***But God hath revealed them unto us by his Spirit:* for the Spirit searcheth all things, yea, the deep things of God.**

1 Corinthians 2:9,10

Phillip

Introduction

Worldwide fascination with "other worldly powers and forces" is increasing.

Media interest in the occult is soaring and lends mysteries to situations, most of which have no answer; hence the desire to explore the *unknown*.

It is popular in our culture to read about:

- Fortune-telling

- Extrasensory Perception

- Transcendental Meditation

- Mental Telepathy

- Soul Travel

- Astral Travel

- Magic

- Tarot Cards

- Ouija Boards

- Parapsychology

- Palm Reading

- Handwriting Analysis

- Clairvoyance

- Fetishes

- Sorcery

- Witchcraft

- New Age

- Animal Sacrifices

- Idol Worship

- Feng Shui

- The great religions of our day:

  - Hinduism

  - Buddhism

  - Islam

  - Lamaism

  - Zoroastrianism

The appetite for answers causes many people to go to the occult for answers, *which the occult does not have.*

Searching for out-of-this-world experiences has led many people into confusion and despair. These experiences provide lofty words of eloquence and human philosophy.

People I encounter say, "After all, we all worship one God, don't we?"

My answer to that is a hearty *"NO! My God has one Son, JESUS CHRIST."*

Other than that, the Bible, which teaches that there is one God—the Father, His Son Jesus Christ and the Holy Spirit—

calls these human philosophies "knowledge of nothing." (1 Cor. 2:2 AMP.)

That same chapter says the wisdom and knowledge of this present age are doomed to pass away, as well as their leaders.

Then I read, "God's wisdom was once hidden but now it is *REVEALED!*"

Revelation knowledge is given "to lift us into *HIS PRESENCE!*"

> *Yet to us God has unveiled and revealed them by and through His Spirit, for the [Holy] Spirit searches diligently, exploring and examining everything, even sounding the profound and bottomless things of God [the divine counsels and things hidden and beyond man's scrutiny.]*
>
> **1 Corinthians 2:10 AMP**

This book presents a multitude of Holy Ghost manifestations in short-story format, to convey our real life experiences that everyone hopes to have.

It is not a book on prayer, although prayer is certainly involved, because much has already been written on the subject of prayer.

Never seeking publicity, but rather shunning it, led Phillip and me into realms of the supernatural we had never experienced. In this book, we record some of these experiences we have had and which, after Phillip's going to glory, I still have.

1

A Sense of *Destiny*

A divine discontent began to possess Phillip and me. A great yearning filled us to be absolutely controlled by the Holy Spirit.

We both worked in our local Assembly of God church since youths but we were in a static place in our Christian experience. The plateau we lived on had no new horizons— everything was maintaining the "status quo" and it seemed all our friends were in exactly that same place.

Then, in 1962, our pastor invited us to join him in opening a downtown mission completely separate from our church. He resigned his pastorate and rented a large (former) burlesque theatre in the center of downtown Minneapolis. This was soon thriving. Every night of the week three balconies were filled and overflowing, producing throngs of seekers for the peace of Jesus. Both Phillip and I worked at the altar and in the prayer room and conducted follow-up teaching for the new converts in "What's Happened to Me" seminars.

Imagine the needs of these dear converts. For some, food and clothing meant survival. Our hearts were touched with the challenge of ministering to these new brothers and sisters.

Both Phillip and I had just been filled with the mighty baptism in the Holy Spirit. I remember so well the day Phillip and I were discussing our budget in relation to our desire to help others. There was not enough money to do both.

We determined that day to take to heart Luke 6:38:

> **Give, and it shall be given unto you; good measure, pressed down, and shaken together, and running over, shall men give into your bosom. For with the same measure that ye mete withal it shall be measured to you again.**

and Malachi 3:10:

> **Bring ye all the tithes into the storehouse, that there may be meat in mine house, and prove me now herewith, saith the Lord of hosts, if I will not open you the windows of heaven, and pour you out a blessing, that there shall not be room enough to receive it.**

A joyous abandonment filled us! We were eager to expand the scope of our lives. Why not immediately begin to tithe as if we already had the increase we wanted in finances? We had never heard of this being done, but we felt like pioneers launching forth into this new dimension.

I know what you could be thinking: SOMEONE DIED AND LEFT US A FORTUNE? We discovered oil in our backyard? We uncovered a cache of diamonds in our attic?

JESUS!!! then: the unique gifts of the Holy Spirit began to operate, and events were set in motion that changed the course of our lives from that day on.

The very first thing that occurred was a very close and intimate fellowship with the Father. Our commitment led us to lean heavily on His breast, feel the heaving of His love and that breath of the Spirit of God becoming so preciously close.

It was a time of awe—to be in the very presence of God! The certain knowledge that He is God of every situation filled us. A sense of destiny to walk in a greater dimension of His Holy Spirit overwhelmed us and became a consuming desire.

Intercessory prayer began to develop and operate, together with the word of wisdom and the word of knowledge. (The word of knowledge pertains to former and present persons, circumstances or events; and the word of wisdom has to do with the future.)

We were to discover miraculous happenings!

And ye shall seek me, and find me, when ye shall search for me with all your heart.

Jeremiah 29:13

2

First Farmhand *Experience*

When Phillip was eighteen years old, all the crops burned out on his family's farm, where there were ten hungry mouths to feed. The whole community was suffering.

One of his cousins had been going to North Dakota to work in the harvest fields in the fall, and he knew a farmer who needed four men to work. He said, "I've got room for one more passenger in my car, but no promise of work."

Phillip said, "I'd like to go." Phillip wanted to be on his own, and he was convinced he should be that passenger.

Phillip borrowed five dollars from his uncle, packed his suitcase and went on what would be his first adventure of the Holy Spirit working in his behalf. Six hundred miles later, his cousin dropped him off by himself in a small North Dakota town before daybreak.

Phillip says he sat on the steps of a small, empty store. He felt very lonely, but he did the only thing he knew how to do: *He prayed!*

Since he had spent most of his money for food on the way, there wasn't any way for him to get back home, so he said he gratefully rested in the presence of God.

Phillip knew God, but at this point in his life, he had not received the baptism of the Holy Spirit.

He asked God to open up a job for him. He didn't have to wait long, for just as the sun was breaking, two men in an old jalopy pulled up right in front of him. They knew of a farmer down the road who needed help.

Phillip gave them his last few cents to drive him down to the farm.

Phillip walked into the farmyard and inquired if they could use some help.

He was told, "Yes, we are going to need a large crew, for our crops are excellent!"

So he put his old suitcase down in the corner of the machine shed and went to work.

When noon came, he was invited into the farmhouse for dinner. The other farmhands were served in the bunkhouse.

Can you imagine how joyful he was when the farmer gave thanks to the Lord for the food and for sending Phillip there?

The farmer announced that they were going to have a church meeting in their house that night and anyone who wanted to come was invited.

Phillip said, "I could see the hand of God leading me and directing me to the home of a Christian."

Of a crew of about twenty men, the only other young man he became acquainted with was Richard Palmer, who later became an outstanding missionary from the Assemblies of

God to Peru. Both Phillip and Richard attended the meeting that night.

After singing and the sermon, they knelt down for a time of earnest prayer.

Phillip watched the people with amazement, and Richard was filled with the Holy Spirit that night.

From the pre-dawn loneliness in a small, unknown town, Phillip now had good food at this family's table, a job, a bed in the house instead of the bunkhouse with the other workers, and he ended the day with Christian fellowship.

Now unto him that is able to do exceeding abundantly above all that we ask or think, according to the power that worketh in us.

Ephesians 3:20

3

Love Was in the Air

From the time that I was twelve, I played the piano for my church.

When I was a senior in high school, I noticed a good-looking young man in the choir.

At this time there were no boys in my life. I led a completely separate life.

I had long hair, braided around my head, and I wore no makeup.

We in the church never went to anything at school because our pastor told us it was worldly, so we had no contact with unbelievers.

At a housewarming for our pastor, Phillip came over and sat right next to me and introduced himself.

Then he asked, "How are you getting home tonight?"

I said, "On the forty-eight passenger (a streetcar)—all five of us—my mother, aunt, sister, brother and myself."

He said, "I'm going your way."

I don't think he knew what my way was, but he was going to take me home. So we piled in his car.

I even asked my girlfriend if she wanted a lift home because she lived so close.

I put her next to Phillip, and then I sat next to her in the front seat.

Phillip dropped Evelyn off and walked up to the door with her; then he dropped all of us off at my house. My mother commented, "What good manners he has!"

That's how he figured out where I lived!

At other times, Phillip would give all five of us a ride home from church.

This led to a friendship. Phillip lived 100 miles away on a farm in Wisconsin and could come to Minneapolis only on weekends.

After a courtship of three years, we married.

Eight months later, Phillip was drafted into the U.S. Army. Nine months after that, Pearl Harbor was bombed, and he served until World War II was over.

When he returned, we established our home in Minneapolis where we were very active in our church, serving in many capacities.

We had been married almost seven years when our son Jim was born.

For this reason a man shall leave his father and his mother and shall be joined to his wife, and the two shall become one flesh.

Ephesians 5:31 AMP

The oneness of our marriage and the commitment of our total lives to Jesus Christ, to be used as He desired, caused us to be a powerful force in prayer against the works of the enemy as we stood in the gap for others.

4

After Phillip's Baptism in the

Holy Spirit

After Phillip was baptized with the Holy Spirit and prayed in tongues, he prayed at home, in church prayer meetings and in home prayer meetings, but he never did anything in the congregation.

We sat together and listened to what was going on. I played the piano for the meetings.

First Corinthians 14:14 says, **For if I pray in an unknown tongue, my spirit prayeth, but my understanding is unfruitful.**

Often Phillip felt led to go on and pray, and while he was praying, he would yield to the urge to speak in tongues. It didn't make any difference where he was. It could be at a job, driving the car, reading his Bible, at the breakfast table, or listening to someone speak.

He would find himself breathing prayers in tongues to God.

Because of teaching we had received, we knew Phillip's prayers were on behalf of other people. He would feel the needs of others as he was praying.

While Phillip was praying in English, utterance in tongues would come forth.

The Holy Spirit, the Helper, assists in our prayers with supernatural utterances.

Romans 8:26-27 says the Holy Spirit meets us and takes hold with us in prayer.

> **Likewise the Spirit also helpeth our infirmities: for we know not what we should pray for as we ought: but the Spirit itself [Himself] maketh intercession for us with groanings which cannot be uttered.**

> **And he that searcheth the hearts knoweth what is the mind of the Spirit, because he maketh intercession for the saints according to the will of God.**

Groanings and words in English would come forth as Phillip prayed in tongues. We were both puzzled. We told our pastor, because we had confidence in him.

He said he had never heard of a similar experience, but he assured us that the Holy Spirit was bringing forth these English words.

> **Howbeit when he, the Spirit of truth, is come, he will guide you into all truth: for he shall not speak of himself; but whatsoever he shall hear, that shall he speak: and he will shew you things to come.**

> **He shall glorify me: for he shall receive of mine, and shall shew it unto you.**

> **John 16:13,14**

The Spirit of truth was dwelling richly in Phillip. I had not received the baptism of the Holy Spirit yet, but I met with Phillip to pray.

I would say to Phillip, "Oh, Phillip, I wish I knew the Spirit like you know the Spirit." And he would say, "I wish I knew the Word like you know the Word." So we were a good combination together!

Phillip's prayer life continued in the most astonishing ways.

5

My *Salvation*

Russell H. Olson, a Baptist pastor, graduated from Northwestern Bible School and took his first pastorate with Tabernacle Baptist Church.

The first summer daily Vacation Bible School he directed was the first time I had ever been in a Baptist church, having been raised and confirmed a Lutheran.

In the Lutheran catechism I learned that the chief end of man is "to glorify God and enjoy Him forever."

But I thought, *None of my Lutheran relatives ever enjoyed God!*

At daily Vacation Bible School, the rewards for learning and privately reciting and identifying Scripture verses were paper airplanes strung over the main sanctuary.

I was delighted to be publicly acknowledged as the winner and to receive my first Bible, which I still have, written in and signed by Pastor Olson.

There was more. I was called into the pastor's office the Saturday before the program, and there I knelt at my pastor's knee and received Jesus as my personal Savior. I will never forget that moment.

In fact, within a few days after Phillip went on to heaven, I drove in my old neighborhood to remind myself of that salvation experience.

I decided to walk in the main doors of what was now Augsburg Seminary. It was being used as a theater training and rehearsal site.

Nevertheless, I found my way to the upper balcony, amid much debris, to the northwest corner "office" Pastor used, with its arch windows.

I just let the tears flow. God's hand has been on me from that very moment at age twelve.

Looking back, it is no wonder that my favorite subject to teach on in the Old Testament is the Tabernacle in the Wilderness.

In that first daily Vacation Bible School craft class, taught by my pastor, we constructed the tabernacle out of white sheets, toothpicks and lots of wallpaper paste!

Much later, after I received the baptism in the Holy Spirit, these images, lessons and meanings came alive to me in a real spiritual sense.

> **As for me, going on the way [of obedience and faith] the Lord led me....**
>
> **Genesis 24:27** AMP

6

Filled to the *Brim*

Phillip and I were so thankful for Brother Kenneth E. Hagin's good advice and counsel, which caused drastic changes in us and led us into a ministry.

In those days Phillip and I were not thinking we would ever be talking to people. So when I talk about ministry, I mean we were helpers with whatever went on. We liked to pray, and that's all.

I had not received the baptism in the Holy Spirit yet. But shortly after that, I was so hungry for the baptism of the Holy Spirit that I cried to the Lord. I'd open my mouth and say, "O Lord, baptize me now with Your Holy Spirit."

I would wait for God to fill me, and of course it didn't come that way. I had not had good teaching in this area.

One day I told Phillip I dreamed I had prayed in tongues all night.

He said, "Well, continue on in prayer as I go to work, and the Lord will fill you today."

So I threw myself across my bed and cried out to the Lord.

I thought of things I had done wrong: I had lied to my father; I had lied to my mother. I told God everything I could think of that was on my mind, why I didn't deserve to pray those holy words that were coming to me.

The last words I said were, "Oh, God, I'm so unworthy."

Immediately God said, *Now you're worthy. You can't ever be worthy enough.*

I just let the words flow out of me, and they came all day.

I got up from the bed and did some things around the house and prepared supper.

I didn't want to quit praying in tongues when Phillip came home, because I thought if I ever stopped, maybe I wouldn't be able to start again.

That began my life in the Spirit with my husband. It was wonderful.

God was leading us into ministry, but we didn't know it, cherish it, want it, crave it or think about it at all.

The word of wisdom and the word of knowledge were coming forth from us, and we learned that we didn't have to understand them.

What a relief! We only had to be obedient to give ourselves to the urge of prayer.

The prayer of the upright is His [the Lord's] **delight!**

Proverbs 15:8 AMP

7

Standing in the *Gap*

Pastor Russell Olson had resigned his long pastorate at Fremont Tabernacle in response to God's direction to begin a downtown Minneapolis mission.

The old burlesque theater off Hennepin Avenue was for lease. I remember the day Pastor Olson came to our house to pray about getting the finances to secure that property for two years.

We had just moved to a house next door, and because the elderly man had not filed his wife's death certificate (as well as other important documents), he told us we could move in and pay him when everything was in order.

Our mortgage money had been approved and we occupied that house for a little over a year before he got everything untangled.

In the meantime, we had over $2000 in the bank from the sale of our house, and when we offered it on a one-year note to Pastor Olson, he tearfully and gratefully accepted. (He repaid our money within six months.)

The Minneapolis Evangelistic Auditorium was such a huge success. Three balconies overflowed with throngs of people. Oral Roberts came for the opening (having been at Fremont Tabernacle some years before with a crowd of thirty-five on a bitterly cold and snowy winter night).

Pastor Olson was the only one we shared our Holy Spirit experiences with. It was he who stopped by and over some coffee told us of a speaker who was coming in two weeks— Kenneth E. Hagin.

The motive of Phillip's heart and mine was to stand in the gap before the Lord for others, encouraging them to move into God's will for their lives.

> **And I sought a man among them who should build up the walls and stand in the gap before Me for the land, that I should not destroy it....**
>
> **Ezekiel 22:30 AMP**

8

We Meet Kenneth E. *Hagin*

We had never heard of Kenneth E. Hagin, but Pastor Olson explained that he had some of the same kind of experiences we had in prayer, so we looked forward to the ten days of meetings.

It was our custom to entertain visiting ministers and Pastor at our home after some evening services, but our pastor said not to plan to include Brother Hagin and his wife. They do not engage in any social activity during meetings, and so they would be staying in their small trailer behind the church.

Both our pastor and Brother Hagin greeted everyone at the entrance, and we took our seats in the congregation.

Brother Hagin had not preached very long when he stopped. Looking directly where we were seated, he asked Phillip to "stand up and pray in the Spirit."

My husband had never stood up in church and said *anything*. He later explained how puzzled he felt. He just stood up and the Holy Spirit gushed out of him in tongues, with great force and power.

The moment he finished, Brother Hagin interpreted. It was a prophecy about a war that was coming and would tear America because of the loss of many American soldiers.

Several years later, the Vietnam War occurred and the prophecy came true.

It was after that first night that Brother Hagin came to us at the close of the meeting and asked us if we four could drive in our car somewhere outside of the metropolitan area and pray together. Certainly we would, and we did.

As Phillip stopped the car, he said, "Brother Hagin, before we go to prayer, I have something I would like to ask you."

"Yes," replied Brother Hagin, "what is it?"

"In the last two or three months, every once in a while when I am praying in tongues, English words will come which I do not understand," Phillip explained. "The words 'cookie' and 'candy' will come. Now, would the Holy Spirit pray about a cookie and a piece of candy?"

Both Brother Hagin and Oretha began to laugh.

"Those are the nicknames of our two granddaughters, Cookie and Candy! They are the children of our daughter Pat and her husband, Buddy Harrison."

How could we know then the scenario that would follow? In just a few months, Buddy and Pat Harrison and Cookie and Candy were at our church. Buddy was installed as youth leader of our downtown mission.

How well I remember playing the piano for his children's choir, which was a place for youth to get together and pray, be filled with the Spirit and speak and sing in tongues.

What a glorious influence they brought to our church in that old movie auditorium!

After that first night of prayer with the Hagins, we met every night after service, sometimes in the car, but mostly at our home, praying in the Spirit. We received much-needed instruction and help from Brother Hagin.

A relationship was established that could not be broken. Phillip and I have always cherished that faithful friendship.

The Holy One, the True One...opens and no one shall shut...shuts and no one shall open.

Revelation 3:7 AMP

9

Getting *Acquainted*

When we heard Brother Hagin was having his first seminar in Tulsa at the Sheridan Assembly of God Church, we drove there and met Billye Brim and Kenneth Copeland (a rather fat young man in an old jalopy, which he later said was "held together with baling wire"!).

We didn't get acquainted with anybody, and it was only after a few years of seeing and hearing about these people that we recognized them at Brother Hagin's meetings.

After that first meeting, Brother and Sister Hagin invited Phillip and me and some others to see their new living quarters above a hall. Up the steps we went to see a modest apartment.

Ushering us past some French doors, Brother Hagin introduced us to Mama and Papa Goodwin (his own pastors for many years). As we approached them, they arose and grabbed our hands and began to prophesy to us.

I will never forget the impact those words had on us. To my amazement I was hearing about "our ministry" and remarkable occurrences, which later would all come true and which I am now sharing with you.

Getting *Acquainted*

The following year we went to Tulsa to be at Brother Hagin's first seminar. After that first morning service, the Hagins invited us to be their guests at lunch. We sat opposite one another in a small booth.

How honored we were to be with them! And as Brother Hagin began to share his heart for a training school of the Spirit in the Tulsa area, we had an immediate quickening of the Holy Spirit to agree with him and receive it as if it were already theirs.

The four of us drove around Tulsa and the surrounding area. Brother Hagin commented on various parcels of land that were for sale, some at sacrifice prices.

Phillip expressed to Brother Hagin a negative impression on all except one of them which was located in Broken Arrow—and it later turned out to be where Rhema is now located!

I remember also how at lunch Brother Hagin asked Phillip to be his prayer leader, or something to that effect, in the meetings.

Phillip hesitated and then said, "I'm very honored to be asked that, Brother Hagin, and I will pray about it and let you know."

At that response, Oretha said, "Well, you know that Kenneth doesn't ask just anybody to work with him."

We did make it a matter of earnest inquiry of the Lord because we had received no direction in that realm.

Our commitment at the very beginning was *to hear directly from God for ourselves, and when we were assured it was God, we would act on it.*

We never had peace about being placed in this position. God continually intercepted our lives with direction and words of knowledge and words of wisdom.

We were at Rhema every opportunity that we had. With Phillip employed by the U.S. government during all these happenings, we used vacation time to pursue what the Lord had spoken and impressed us to do.

Phillip would never take sick leave. First, he was never sick. In fact, all the years we were married, I would occasionally have a cold or a feeling of malaise or tiredness from going so much, but Phillip didn't have those symptoms at all.

Later, when Phillip took an early retirement, he was compensated for every day of sick leave he had accumulated, at the current rate of pay. What a blessing this was to us!

The many times Brother Hagin would call us out—with others—to prophesy to us, are memorable. The same things that the Holy Spirit had been uttering in our lips, we heard confirmed—or often we heard it for the first time from Brother Hagin, and it would be confirmed to us later.

Remember the first thing that Mary did after the angel Gabriel declared to her that she would conceive and bear the Messiah, and that her cousin Elizabeth was six months pregnant?

Immediately, she journeyed to see Elizabeth, and there she found the confirmation she needed for her own peace.

When you know God has spoken to you, act immediately.

Our commitment was very similar to that of Paul, who said:

But when He, Who had chosen and set me apart [even] before I was born and had called me by His grace (His undeserved favor and blessing), saw fit and was pleased to reveal (unveil, disclose) His Son within me so that I might proclaim Him among the Gentiles (the non-Jewish world) as the glad tidings (Gospel), immediately I did not confer with flesh and blood [did not consult or counsel with any frail human being or communicate with anyone].

Galatians 1:15,16 AMP

10

Santals

The very first experience Phillip and I had with the direct leading of the Holy Spirit through prayer was discovering the part our prayers and actions played in seeing a manifestation of the Holy Spirit.

"Santals! Santals!" Over and over again during prayer, and interspersed during the day for three or four days, that forceful word came through Phillip.

It had no meaning to us. All I could think of was a sandalwood soap I formerly used. So I consulted the dictionary; it proved to be of no help as it identified "santal" as sandalwood.[1]

I got the idea to look in the telephone book for Santal. I found one listing—"The Santal Mission."

It was located about three miles from our home, so I told Phillip I would drive over the next day and find out all about this mission.

I walked up a flight of dark stairs to a small office where three or four people welcomed me. I described how the Holy Spirit was interrupting our prayers with the word *Santals.*

"Oh!" they exclaimed. *"Did you not know about our Santal tribe? Did you not know they are being overrun with bandits?"*

This tribe of people—the Santals—were on the border of Tibet and China, and they were being attacked by vicious northern Chinese bandits.

With the assurance that the Holy Spirit was actively working on their behalf, we spent a little while in prayer and wonderment.

Their thanks and appreciation were profuse and their spirits were enlightened!

The Holy Spirit intervened. No need for further alarm. Just rejoice in His rescue and defense.

Whatever the outcome, God had stepped in for His purposes. Hallelujah!

I will not be afraid of ten thousands of people, that have set themselves against me round about.

Psalm 3:6

Now, what part did our prayers and actions play?

Trouble was approaching rapidly to these precious Lutheran missionaries to the Santal people. An alert was sounded in heaven.

I can picture Michael, the warring angel, uttering the name "Santal," alerting all heaven to bring deliverance.

This was translated to be sounded on earth in a loud, declarative and commanding way—*"Santals! Santals!"*

It certainly got our attention.

The encouragement, blessing and comfort my visit and transmission of God's intervention brought to these people encouraged Phillip and me to be aware of words spoken to us by His Spirit.

There are, it may be, so many kinds of voices in the world, and none of them is without signification.

1 Corinthians 14:10

11

Larry

I was in a cleaning mood that memorable day.

While vacuuming in the dining room and moving the chairs, I was listening to Christian radio.

I heard the announcer tell of Larry, a thirteen-year-old boy who, along with a baby sibling, was taken out of his home because of parental neglect.

School authorities had found Larry feeding the baby cookies, the only food in the house.

Larry needed a home for a couple of days until they could place him in a Christian foster home. If not placed, he would have to go in with some troubled youths in a detention home.

"Please call this number," the announcer pleaded, "if you have room for a couple of nights."

I had a thirteen-year-old son in a room with twin beds.

I could imagine his switchboard lighting up with dozens of calls from all over Minneapolis and St. Paul.

Over and over the plea came forth as I polished my house.

I wondered why people didn't call in, since we have a very large evangelical community in the Twin Cities.

I couldn't stand it any longer. I called.

Yes, I could have this boy for a couple of nights. I invited the social worker to bring Larry over so they could have supper with us to "break the ice."

Smiling brightly alongside the social worker, whom I'll call Mr. Oaks, and coming up our walk was a very fine-looking boy who was the same height as our own son.

The legs of his jeans were way too short, the crotch too tight and the shirt much too small. He wore no stockings and had holes in his tennies, and I'll spare you the description of his underwear, which I threw out!

I had made spaghetti and meatballs, vegetables and salad for supper. The five of us sat around our kitchen table getting acquainted as we ate.

While our son, Jim, was showing Larry their room, Mr. Oaks wanted to talk to us privately.

Larry had a bed-wetting problem related to his emotional stress. It was thought wise to withhold liquids after supper and also to get him up during the night.

I prepared the bed, putting an old oilcloth under his sheet, and never mentioned the problem.

After Mr. Oaks left, Phillip and I brought the boys to our living room for our evening devotions.

Sometimes Jim would read whatever verses or passage of Scripture he wanted, and sometimes he led us in prayer.

We didn't have a set format.

That night a quiet Larry sat in the big wing-back chair and just studied us as we worshipped the Lord.

We didn't manage to catch Larry that first night before he wet the bed.

After a quick shower and clean pajamas, he got back into a clean bed.

We faithfully kept liquids away from him after supper and got him up at night, but frequently by morning he had still wet the bed. We never mentioned it to him.

Our son declared he was not sleeping in that room anymore.

Rivalry developed between Jim and Larry, due to the fact that Larry needed a lot of attention from me, and this was attention Jim had never had to share before.

They dug a deep gouge in the desk, dividing Larry's side of the room from Jim's side. Neither was to cross it!

I had many occasions to call Mr. Oaks, as a couple of days became a couple of weeks. I had to enroll Larry in school until a foster home could be found.

Larry went with us to Sunday school and church, of course, but seemed hesitant to respond to altar calls.

We so wanted him of his own volition to want Jesus that we put no pressure on him to accept Jesus right away.

I guess we wanted him to see Jesus in us and want Him.

It was Good Friday night and Phillip was reading the story of Pilate's refusing Jesus—"Good" Friday for us, but "bad" Friday for Jesus.

Phillip stressed the necessity of making the right decision and accepting Jesus for who He said He was—our Savior.

We three got down on our knees to pray. (Larry never did this with us.)

I've forgotten which one of us was praying, when we heard loud sobs coming from across the living room.

We all crawled over to Larry to hear him tell us, sobbing, he didn't want to refuse Jesus!

After our prayer with him, we rejoiced that this date, April 20, was his *real* birthday.

"Let's celebrate Larry's birthday!" we all cried.

Phillip popped popcorn (a luxury we had never allowed at night, for Larry's sake, since we always had root beer with it).

I got the root beer ready, and as we sat together in a very joyful mood, Larry said, "Remember, I can't have any liquids."

Phillip said, "But, Larry, you are now a new creation as we read in the Bible. Old and former things have passed away, and all things have become new. You are not going to have any problem from now on with liquids at night."

Each of us had a couple of glasses of root beer with our popcorn and had a wonderful, fun time together!

Larry remained with us for several more weeks. He never wet the bed again.

> **For I will restore health unto thee, and I will heal thee of thy wounds, saith the Lord....**
>
> **Jeremiah 30:17**

12

Beverly Road *Home*

On our way home from Sunday morning service, Phillip turned to the right on a side street.

"What are you doing? Where are you going? I have dinner on, and we need to get home," I declared.

Although we were only across a bridge to our home in Minneapolis, less than a mile away, Phillip informed me he had seen a "garage sale" sign.

"We never go to garage sales on Sunday, Phillip," I reminded him.

The fifth house had their garage door wide open and a small "garage sale" sign was on the lawn. Phillip pulled into the driveway.

The garage looked empty, with a couple of empty tables, and no one was there.

As he got out of the car, an older lady and a gentleman came from their kitchen and greeted us.

"Is this the place for a 'garage sale'?" Phillip inquired.

"Yes, but we haven't got the stuff out yet," replied the gentleman.

"Can I help you?" was my response, although I knew I had to get home to my pot roast.

"Thank you," the woman said and led me inside. We went to a walkout downstairs with huge windows.

"Oh! What am I looking at? I don't know where I am right now!" I exclaimed.

There in front of me was the most beautiful display of nature's magnificence I had ever seen.

"You are looking across the Mississippi River at Minneapolis. You should see it at night," she said.

I helped her with a pile of men's clothing. "These belonged to my husband, who died a year ago, and I need to get rid of them!" was her emphatic statement.

"Oh, Phillip!" I exclaimed. "Do you know where we are? On the edge of this high point in St. Paul, you can see way into Minneapolis with all the glorious fall colors." This was mid-October.

"Come on in," they urged us. "See the view for yourselves from our living room windows."

We stood in awe of the large glass, almost-floor-to-ceiling Pella windows. We didn't realize we were up so high, just driving to and from church on a nearby street. The view was spectacular.

We were told that an old doctor who lived three doors south had determined this to be the highest point on this stretch of the Mississippi River.

"You should see it in winter," they offered. "It is like a fairyland; and that gigantic oak tree was sculptured eighteen years ago when I built the house. I hired Bachman's to do the yard. Everyone admires that tree in every season."

Coming back into the garage, we thanked them for showing us the view and Phillip noticed a long box on the table. "What is that?" he inquired.

"It's a hedge trimmer, and it's never been out of the box," said the gentleman, Mr. Hardin.

The price on it was marked $59.95, and he offered it to Phillip for $10—never used!

"Phillip," I volunteered, "we don't even have a hedge to trim."

"Well, for that price," said Phillip, "I'll give it as a gift to someone who does."

Thanking them, we left for the mile drive across the Mississippi bridge.

No sooner had we opened our door than the telephone rang. "Mrs. Halverson?" inquired the voice.

"Yes. Who is this?" I asked.

"This is Mr. Hardin. You were just in my home and you left your purse on my car trunk in the driveway. I took the liberty to find your identification and let you know your purse is safe."

I was so surprised! How nice of these people! Phillip drove over to get my purse while I finished the dinner preparations.

Neither one of us dreamed we would ever see these people again.

About a week later, going to a dental appointment, I parked my car in front of a large, well-known furniture store. Locking my car, I saw a man waving and motioning for me to come in. It was Mr. Hardin, the man on whose car trunk I'd left my purse!

Stopping for a moment, he greeted me warmly, and with enthusiasm he said he and his wife wanted us to come over soon—they would call us.

I didn't give it much thought. However, a phone call the next day from them was an invitation to come over that evening.

I must admit I was curious to see the rest of the house, as they suggested.

We also would have an opportunity for the Holy Spirit to open the conversation regarding their eternal welfare.

The dining room table was laden with homemade candies: dark and light fudge, peanut butter fudge, peanut brittle, fondant, strawberries dipped in chocolate and popcorn balls. They were both diabetic but kept candy around for emergencies, they said.

"What a large and beautiful music room," I said.

"This is really the master bedroom, but with the grand piano, we decided to keep this a special place for our music and musical groups," stated Mr. Hardin.

We marveled at the huge stone fireplace in the overly large living room and the state-of-the-art kitchen.

Another bedroom on the main floor was their bedroom; and a beautifully tiled bathroom with separate tub and shower and a large, long vanity was quite a showpiece in itself.

The garage was attached, and one entered into a hallway and then into the kitchen or hall to the front door and living room. The abundance of cabinets, built-in storage all over with "his" and "her" large wardrobes, was a wonder to me.

The walkout was equally large and even had a small kitchen—really it was suitable for an apartment on its own.

As we enjoyed refreshments with them, we complimented them on their fine home and the many innovative ideas they had incorporated.

Mr. Hardin assured us that he'd built the house with a prominent local architect's plans for that overlook lot and the contractor was recognized for his upscale houses in the area. We were amazed.

As we commented on their good taste (Mr. Hardin was the owner of the furniture store I'd parked in front of!), suddenly he pointed his finger at Phillip.

"Mr. Halverson, I am going to sell you this house!" Phillip just smiled broadly and I, thinking this surely was some kind of joke, smiled in derision.

On our way across the bridge to our Minneapolis home a mile away, Phillip said, "That is the kind of a house I like."

After all the times I had tried to get Phillip to stop for some "Open House" viewing, and after all the times he had said, "We've got a nice house and have done everything we can do to improve it for eighteen years. I don't want to stop and look at anything!"

But now that he had seen a house no doubt far beyond our lifestyle, he liked it! *Anyone* would love that house! I was amused but didn't say anything.

I never thought we would see the Hardins again—we had no reason.

But three or four days later, Mr. Hardin called and asked us if we could stop over. I knew this was another opportunity to share Jesus, which we hadn't had on the previous visit.

"Sure, tell him we'll be over about seven o'clock," said Phillip.

We were welcomed enthusiastically.

Mr. Hardin had a large stack of files on the raised fireplace hearth and methodically went through them to show us what he had put into this home. We sat in silence as the staggering total became apparent.

"My wife died three years ago, and Honey's husband just passed away. We were very good friends, and Honey and I married only a short time ago," related Mr. Hardin.

"I have owned the furniture store for thirty years," he continued, "and I am being asked every month to sell out to four of my top salesmen.

"Honey has been around the world four times, and now we believe we will sell out and kick up our heels in whatever years we have left to live in Scottsdale, Arizona, instead of here."

Very interesting, I thought, wondering why he was going over all this with us.

It was the perfect opportunity. We spoke of the brevity of life and what's beyond it. After almost an hour we had the wonderful privilege of leading them to the foot of the cross, where they confessed their need of the Savior. They'd had a strict and faithful Episcopalian upbringing.

We thanked them for their hospitality and such an interesting time.

As we headed out the door, Mr. Hardin took Phillip's hand and said, very seriously, "Mr. Halverson, I am going to sell you my home!"

Phillip's response was only a big smile and a handshake.

As soon as we drove home, I asked Phillip, "Why didn't you tell him we are *not* in the market for his house?

"Sure, it's a great and wonderful house, but it's far, far beyond anything we would even dream of. This man is serious, Phillip, and you should call him and at least settle his thinking of us as prospects. We are not prospects at all."

Arriving home, I continued to insist that Phillip let them know that they were talking to the wrong people. We could never afford that home, and we were not looking.

Our Minneapolis home was very nice. Add to that the fact that it was very difficult to save money to make the twice-yearly farm payments so we wouldn't lose our total investment in the farm.

Phillip listened to me and said nothing.

I never believed we would ever enter that house again or talk face-to-face with Mr. and Mrs. Hardin.

Several days later the telephone rang, and it was Mr. Hardin.

"I want to stop by your home for a few minutes. Is that all right?" he asked.

Why in the world would he stop by? He had our address and Phillip was not home, but I told him it was okay.

This was the first part of November, and we had a good two feet of snow.

Then Phillip came home, and I informed him of my dilemma.

Our son Jim had just broken his engagement to a lovely Catholic girl. (She was born again when Jim led her to the Lord.) Jim had asked us if he could move back home for a couple of weeks until he could find an apartment.

When I arrived home late that afternoon, just before Mr. Hardin had called, I could hardly get in my front door. Jim had brought a lot of furniture and my dining room was full of it—bed, dresser, chest, spring and mattress, end tables, lamps, sofa and love seat.

I had expected him to move back a couple of bookcases, his stereo and clothes to the downstairs, where he'd had his space while attending the university. He explained to me, and I now explained to Phillip.

We had to literally make a path through our living room to get into the rest of the house.

The doorbell rang, and there stood Mr. Hardin.

"Are you folks moving?" he asked in disbelief at what he saw.

I explained what had happened, and he said, "There is a 'For Sale' sign in front of your house!"

In utter disbelief, I ran out to the porch. There, stuck in the snow, was a realtor's "For Sale" sign. As it turned out, it belonged to the house next door. I walked in the deep snow with my shoes on and moved the "For Sale" sign to the porch.

Returning, and embarrassed at what Mr. Hardin must have been thinking, I invited him to be seated.

"Honey and I are going to Chicago for the annual furniture exhibition for dealers. We have gone for thirty years to keep up with the latest trends in furniture."

It was now the first part of November. "We have decided to sell the furniture store to the four older salesmen and, Mr. Halverson, when I return in a week from Chicago, *I want you to give me a purchase agreement for my house!*"

We both looked hard at Mr. Hardin. Didn't he get the message? We were in no shape to buy *any* house. We had a nice home, and we were obligated to meet large farm payments. Neither of us said anything.

As abruptly as he had arrived, he left with these words: "I will be here after Chicago to pick up your purchase agreement."

"Is he senile?" I inquired of Phillip. "Doesn't he get the message that we are definitely *not* buyers for his house—or for any house?"

I was not prepared for Phillip's response:

"We have a purchase agreement in the desk. Why don't you get it out, and we'll look it over."

Stunned, and as if in an unreal dream, I sat at the kitchen table.

We had $1,600 in a savings account for the next annual payment on the farm, and we needed more than twice that amount in about four months.

"What do you want to put down for earnest money?" I very weakly asked.

"Put $1,600," instructed Phillip. I felt physically sick and weak.

There was no doubt about it: We would lose our investment in the farm. Out the window! Gone!

When I heard Phillip say we would offer only $39,000 for this house, *I CHANGED TO HAPPY!*

Phillip put the signed agreement in an envelope and placed it on the fireplace mantel. It stayed there, not even thought about, until a week later.

"Hello, Halversons!" said a cheery voice on the phone. "Honey and I just got in from Chicago, and I'd like to stop by and pick up the purchase agreement."

"We are home, and you are welcome to stop by," Phillip responded.

In a few minutes, Mr. Hardin arrived in the snowstorm. and after some remarks about the flight and precarious landing, he sat, hat in hand, his overcoat still on, and proceeded to tell us about the furniture show.

"I've never seen anything like it," he said. "Salesmen I've known and ordered from for many years begged me for orders. Even just a confirmation order would be great for them to take back to their companies."

He repeated several times that he had never seen anything like it.

"I made up my mind I am going to sell out the furniture business to my salesmen who have been wanting to buy it for some time, sell my home, and Honey and I will kick up our heels and enjoy life in a warmer climate.

"Do you have the purchase agreement?" he inquired.

Phillip handed him the sealed envelope from the fireplace mantel. I was holding my breath. I hoped he would not open it in our house. I pictured him seeing it and becoming very angry. I was afraid of what might happen.

He buttoned his overcoat, put on his hat and proceeded out the door with a "Good night" and with the sealed envelope. I was grateful for that.

How he could have gone the mile across the Minneapolis-St. Paul bridge to his house and called so quickly, I do not know. The phone rang, and I answered it.

"Well, folks, you have just bought yourselves a nice home!" was Mr. Hardin's cheery, enthusiastic comment.

"Oh, Mr. Hardin," I exclaimed quickly, "don't sign it! It is a legal document. Don't sign it."

I was sure he would give it to his attorney, and the attorney would give him four times that price. My mind was awhirl.

"Oh, my, we think it is just fine. Honey and I just signed it, and we thank you. You are just the right people we wanted to sell to," said Mr. Hardin.

That's when the bottom fell out from my faith. We could *not* afford to buy anything. Good-bye to the money we had invested in the farm. Everything was sunk!

We met with them to settle on the closing date, which they wanted to be February 14 of the next year, 1971. (They were married on Valentine's Day.)

They were so relieved to have the house sold, and Mr. Hardin knew his proposal to sell his business would be welcomed. He flung out his arms toward the large floor-to-ceiling windows with the magnificent winter scene and told us:

"We have so much money we could stand out on the deck and throw out ten-dollar bills for a long time just to use up some of our surplus."

They were exuberant and insisted they take us out for a nice dinner at the St. Paul Hotel.

Remember, we had committed our $1,600 for the farm payment to make the down payment on this house. I didn't crave this big, expensive home. I couldn't imagine our furniture fitting in, and to drape or curtain the windows would be a major job.

I was right! Our furniture would look like doll furniture in those big rooms. It was at this point that things began to happen in order for God to bless us—unbeknownst to me. I was completely in the dark, so to speak, and dragged my feet on the whole thing.

For the Lord God is a Sun and Shield; the Lord bestows [present] grace and favor and [future] glory (honor, splendor, and heavenly bliss)! No good thing will He withhold from those who walk uprightly.

O Lord of hosts, blessed (happy, fortunate, to be envied) is the man who trusts in You [leaning and believing on You, committing all and confidently looking to You, and that without fear or misgiving]!

Psalm 84:11,12 AMP

13

Just in *Time*

Eager to be out in our backyard that first spring in our new home, we were identifying the bushes and bulbs that were coming to life.

We had moved in on Valentine's Day when everything was covered with snow.

"We have a stone patio!" I exclaimed, in wonderment at my discovery.

"And look," Phillip pointed out, "a beautiful stone outdoor fireplace in the far corner of the yard!"

We looked beyond the backyard to a steep bank that was full of growth.

The people from whom we had purchased the home had Bachman's (local and prominent gardeners) build the terraces, plant the shrubs and even sculpt a huge oak tree—a spectacle in the winter snow!

While we were wandering about, our next-door neighbors came over to meet us.

"We are Marguerite and Ward Ingersoll," they announced as they extended their hands to us. "Welcome to the neighborhood!"

"Thank you so much," we responded warmly, commenting on how wonderful it was to be outside after such a severe winter, with it now being the middle of April.

"Our house was built in 1920," stated Mr. Ingersoll, "and we raised our two daughters in this home." He pointed out the very wide and majestic stone fireplace with its double-wide chimney, as well as the steeply roofed third-floor attic.

"We have admired your architecture since the first time we saw it," was Phillip's comment.

"Come on in and see it for yourselves," they invited. We accepted eagerly.

"We lived in the basement while we were building the house. In fact," Ward continued, "we have two basements."

From bottom to top, we viewed the home with its expansive rooms and attic. All had exquisite details that spoke of the home's prestige. Ward and Marguerite proudly showed off their life's dream.

"Does your family live near?" I inquired.

"No," they responded, "both daughters live on the West Coast, and we see them infrequently."

It was at that moment that I realized these were two elderly people who were very alone.

Our kitchen window overlooked part of their beautiful yard. I had noticed Marguerite step outside the back entrance at their walkout basement to smoke a cigarette occasionally during the few months we had been there.

We were happy to make their acquaintance. They had many things to tell us about the history of the whole neighborhood, about the lot our house stood on and so forth.

The neighbors south of us decided to have a neighborhood welcoming party for us—a cocktail party!

I put my hand over one end of the phone and said, "Phillip, our new neighbors next door want to have a cocktail party for us next Sunday afternoon."

He shook his head no.

I said, "Oh, thank you. What time does it start?"

They said, "Two o'clock."

I said, "We'll be there!"

Phillip just shook his head and walked out of the room.

We went over to their home for the cocktail party.

They greeted us at the door. In the foyer they had a bar set up. I asked, "Do you have Seven-up?"

"Sure." They asked, "Don't you want anything with it?"

I said, "No, I really don't. Thank you."

Phillip said, "I'll have the same."

The host said, "These folks will just have Seven-up."

I said, "We have already had some new wine."

They all looked at us and said, "New? Did you have wine before you got here?"

I said, "Oh, we had new wine at church. The things of the Holy Spirit are new wine."

I couldn't believe I was saying this to these people.

We had a good time and visited with everyone, shook their hands and invited them to stop over anytime they were out walking.

That's how we became acquainted in the neighborhood.

I found out many of the neighbors' birthdays, and on each special day, I'd have cake, coffee or tea. No big deal! They liked to be together.

Then, of course, this was an opportunity to show kindness to them.

Later, seeing the Ingersolls out in the backyard, I invited them to come in and have some soup with us for lunch.

As we sat facing each other at the table, Phillip said, "Let us give thanks for the food." He proceeded with his blessing, not only on the food but on our neighbors.

"We are atheists!" Mr. Ingersoll stiffly announced.

"There is no such thing as an atheist!" I countered. "If you have ever been in the emergency ward of a hospital, you hear everyone there calling on God Almighty!

I surprised myself by my own words. I never had thought of such a thing before.

We had the opportunity to share with them the joy and peace that knowing Jesus Christ personally brings, the satisfaction that everything is finally settled when He is Lord of your life.

Aware that they had thought about their own mortality as each year passed, we had precious moments with them not only that initial time, but many times after that as we shared coffee and cookies at our house and theirs.

Much later, other neighbors whispered to us, "The Ingersolls never have anything to do with the rest of us. They keep to themselves."

I couldn't remember seeing them at the cocktail party.

In the long winding block where we lived, facing the Mississippi River, all of the homes, some of which still housed the original owners who had built them years before, were very nice, but not so imposing as the Ingersolls.

They all lived in their homes until they were so old they had to be taken care of, or they died there and now new families with children had moved in.

The years passed. Phillip left his job with the government to take an early retirement to enter ministry.

Eventually we bought a house in Tulsa, spending eight winters there.

Every time we would leave, Ward and Marguerite were on hand to bid us "good-bye" or "welcome home" in the spring.

One morning in Tulsa over our breakfast, Phillip said, "I have been praying a lot in the Spirit, interceding for the Ingersolls." This kept on frequently for two or three days.

"We have to go up to Minnesota," Phillip informed me, "because I have a great urgency to be with the Ingersolls, and our time is open for over a week."

Of course I agreed, even though this was March and we never left to go North until about May 1.

It didn't take us long to get our clothes packed and the car checked and gassed up for the trip. We took off for Minnesota on a quest we did not know.

"Dad," our son Jim had said in our last phone conversation, "I stopped in to see the Ingersolls. Mrs. Ingersoll is bedridden."

He informed us that he had put his arms around her frail body and had given her a hug and a kiss on her cheek, only to see a tear in her eye. Something was cooking.

Upon arrival at our home, we found out both of them had been placed in a nursing home on the west side of Minneapolis a few days earlier by one of their daughters who had just departed for her West Coast home.

We verified their presence at this nursing home and hightailed it there the morning after we arrived.

We found Marguerite in a two-bed room. Around the corner and down the long hall, Ward was in a bed, also in a two-bed room.

A nurse was just straightening the room and informed us, "Marguerite doesn't respond to anyone. She keeps her eyes closed, and she will not eat anything."

The nurse left the room. We walked over to her bed, and I leaned way down to her.

"Marguerite!" I said loudly, as I pushed back her beautiful white hair covering her left ear. "This is Fern and Phillip

Halverson, your next-door neighbors!" I exclaimed. "We have come to pray with you."

She opened her eyes, lifted up her frail, bony arm and put it on my neck. I was amazed but continued, "Thank You, Lord Jesus, for my friend, Marguerite."

I prayed, "Now as Marguerite opens up her heart and welcomes You, let the angels of heaven minister to her and, dear Lord, usher her into the presence of the Father, in Jesus' name. Amen."

I kissed her, and Phillip and I walked out quietly.

Finding Ward's room, we saw him fully dressed, lying on top of the covers. The attending nurse informed us, "He has a brain tumor and jerks his head wildly, not recognizing anyone."

"Ward!" Phillip called out close to his ear. "Do you know who this is?"

He moved his head toward us and opened his eyes! "My neighbors, Phillip and Fern!" he exclaimed.

"Dear Father," Phillip prayed, placing his hands on Ward's head, "let the angels of heaven minister to Ward right now as he opens his heart to You, Lord Jesus."

Phillip continued, "And, Father, may the heavenly hosts usher Ward into Your very presence, in Jesus' precious name. Amen."

He hugged Ward and left without another word.

Getting back into our car, we had such a sense of accomplishment. We were astonished at the response of each of them. *We knew they were fully conscious and heard us. We were so amazed that God had let us be witness to this!*

Two days later as we were planning our trip back to Tulsa, our phone rang. It was Mary, one of their daughters, who lived in the state of Washington.

"I just wanted you to know that Mom and Dad passed away very quietly night before last in a nursing home." She didn't know we had been there that very day.

After inquiring further, she thanked us for visiting them and thought it was remarkable that *they had passed away just before midnight the very day we had been there!*

God has His own time. We didn't know much, except to follow and do what we were impressed to do.

We marveled at this all the way back to Tulsa, worshipping our God, who can coordinate everything perfectly if we are *willing* and make ourselves available.

What are a couple of thousand earth miles compared to God's lightning speed of accomplishment?

Call unto me, and I will answer thee, and shew thee great and mighty things, which thou knowest not.

Jeremiah 33:3

14

The Bankruptcy *Sale*

Getting settled in our new home, I told Phillip our furniture looked like "doll house furniture" in the big rooms. However, I was not about to go out and buy new furnishings!

On our new routes, I would regularly pass a huge warehouse on University Avenue. I noticed a sign covering one of the huge windows: BANKRUPTCY SALE!

I didn't know or care what a sale like that might be; and thinking of it as one more ploy to sell something, I had no intention of stopping.

I passed this large building many times.

One day as I was preparing to turn, instead of turning I pulled over to the curb right in front of the warehouse and was impressed to walk in.

At one of the two wide front glass doors was a long table, and three or four handsomely dressed businessmen welcomed me to come in and shop.

"Have you ever been to a bankruptcy sale?" one of them asked.

"No, I haven't," was my reply.

"Well, let me explain what this is all about," said one. "We are the manufacturers of the furniture they have here. They have not been able to pay us, so we are here by order of the court to collect whatever we can for the goods on the premises." (This was a three-story building.)

"This is the last day," he stated. One of the gentlemen had a legal-sized pad and a pen and, having invited me to view their goods, asked me, "What are you in the market for— living room, bedroom, dining room furniture?"

"No," I said, "I am just looking."

"Remember, this is the last day of the bankruptcy sale. We will take whatever we can get for any merchandise you select, but it must be out of here by midnight tonight."

There was a lot of furniture on the main floor: beautiful gold-framed, elaborate mirrors, as well as sofas, tables, lamps and more.

Each time I stopped to admire something, the man wrote it down on his legal pad. "Oh, and a gorgeous coffee table over there!" He wrote it down.

"Please don't write an order for me," I said. "I am just admiring your furniture."

He replied, "I have those things down here. And remember, we *have to take whatever you offer today,* because this is the last day under the court order. Everything you select has to be out by midnight," he explained again.

We took the huge freight elevator up to the second floor, which held bedroom furniture, mattresses, springs and so forth.

Then we went to the third floor, where lovely dining room sets were arranged.

When we reached the main floor, I noticed the long list he had marked down with the original prices from their tickets.

Again he told me, "Whatever you want to offer for everything, we will take; but it has to be out of here by midnight tonight."

I wrote him a check for $320 for everything and hurried home to meet Phillip so he could arrange to get the furniture.

We didn't eat supper that evening. Instead, Phillip and our son, Jim, and two friends who had trucks picked up the new furniture and brought it to our house.

We gave away our old furnishings and found out that God not only wanted to give us a beautiful home, but He also wanted to provide brand-new furnishings for it!

What eye has not seen and ear has not heard and has not entered into the heart of man, [all that] God has prepared (made and keeps ready) for those who love Him [who hold Him in affectionate reverence, promptly obeying Him and gratefully recognizing the benefits He has bestowed].

Yet to us God has unveiled and revealed them by and through His Spirit....

1 Corinthians 2:9,10 AMP

15

A Business for *God*

The Lord had blessed me in my work with those who are hard-of-hearing, especially with children.

When the company I worked for in Minneapolis announced that they were going to close their St. Paul office due to a poor investment return, something stirred within me.

Although the firm I was with was very nice to me, I longed for my own business so I would not be tied to unbelieving people and so my customers would have no pressure to buy.

Phillip and I discussed this possibility. It was in the Hamm Building, a prominent office building in the heart of downtown St. Paul. In fact, on the fourth floor there was a walkway to Minnesota's largest department store, Dayton's.

As we laid this before the Lord, we purposed to let God run the business. *It would be His business!* We would only be a *front* for people to get help—physically and spiritually—with emphasis on the spiritual aspect of our commitment.

We would be a true witness to the lost, leading them to salvation and testifying to the blessings of the baptism in the Holy Spirit.

The Minneapolis firm was anxious to be rid of the business. Many of their customers had not paid their bills. There were only six dollars in the company account, and the first of the month was approaching, when they needed to give their thirty-day notice to vacate.

I arranged with them to pay the rent and the telephone for that month and agreed that I would not solicit or advertise in Minneapolis for one year.

The office was a mess, and after some painting and fabric hanging, I put an announcement in the St. Paul paper for an "Open House."

I got out my best silver service and trays and loaded them with cookies, bars, nuts and mints—and my husband bought me an orchid!

My mother helped with the baking and preparations, and we were ready at 2 P.M. sharp that Sunday afternoon for "Open House."

No one showed up!

Yet we had that happy, peaceful feeling that comes with having done the will of God. We were certain that we were in the right place at the right time.

I arrived for my first day in the freshly decorated office at 8:30 the next morning, ready for whatever customers the Lord would send.

I had the office door open and could see people coming from the elevator, heading toward me, but turning the corner to go into Dayton's Department Store.

About 9:30 a gentleman walked into my office. I was typing a letter to my sister, and when I looked up to greet him with, "Can I help you?" he replied, "I have come to pay a bill. I am the executor of my uncle's estate, and I am going around paying his bills."

When I learned the uncle's name, I went into the back room of my four-room space and opened a large ledger for the first time. I found his name, which was redlined with many others, indicating that the company had already written off his account as "uncollectible."

There was his uncle's name, and he owed $600. When I returned to my desk, this gentleman was counting out $50 bills on the counter. He informed me, "My uncle's bill is $600. Right?"

I said, "Correct."

Now, if he had offered to settle that bill for any lesser amount, I would have agreed. We were not there to make money. We were there to be at the Lord's disposal. What a difference!

He counted out the whole $600 and asked me to verify it. I gave him a receipt marked "paid in full," and he left.

We began that first day of business with $6 in the company account. At the end of that day we had $606. God increased His investment by 100 times!

We hadn't done one thing, except to obey the clear impressions to make ourselves available and to keep our motives right.

We began to receive referrals from customers who sent people in from Minneapolis. I felt led to split hours between

St. Paul and some smaller Minneapolis location to better serve the customers.

> **The Lord shall command the blessing upon you in your storehouse and in all that you undertake....**
>
> **Deuteronomy 28:8** AMP

God used supernatural ways to bless this business.

16

Bizarre *Interruptions*

The numerous opportunities and privileges I had to lead people to the Savior in that office are memorable. I will share some of these bizarre Holy Ghost interruptions.

I heard Phillip praying in the Spirit as he lay beside me one night: "E.T. must call...E.T....E.T....E.T. must call..." and some other unconnected words. (I thought this could be referring to my Aunt Emily Tuttle.)

In the office the next morning, I received a phone call from a woman who wanted an appointment for a hearing test.

She came in about 11 A.M. with a friend, and after the hearing evaluation, she asked if she could take the test with her.

Of course, my natural mind told me she would shop around and someone else would talk her into buying a hearing aid. I got busy with other things, had lunch and returned to the office.

She arrived shortly with her friend Edna and told me she had decided to order her hearing aid. As I asked her name, she said, "My name is *Emily Tufts!*"

It wasn't until I was relating this later to Phillip that he said, "That's the E.T. that the Holy Spirit was praying about last night!" And he continued, "That's not the end of it...."

About two weeks later, Edna, the woman who had accompanied Emily, appeared with her husband, Emil, to get a hearing test. He bought one and then disclosed his full name, *Emil Torres*. Another "E.T."

How mysteriously the Holy Ghost works. We had at least another six or seven people appear to be tested and buy instruments whose initials were "E.T."

In another unrelated incident, an elderly and very distinguished white-haired gentleman and his beautiful but frail wife came into my office one afternoon to get a hearing test.

He had a very large "pocket aid" with a long cord and heavy battery, which was wearing out, and he was shopping for a new one.

"The hearing test is free, and there is no pressure to buy in this office," I announced.

Once the test was completed, I recommended a Danish instrument—very powerful and expensive, the only one of twenty brands I could order that would meet his hearing requirements.

I never kept any stock on hand, except for some old trade-ins which I had inherited and which I gave away.

"Reverend Armstrong is my name," he informed me. "I am a Presbyterian minister of over forty-five years."

Oh! I thought. *How wonderful to meet a Christian minister!* We had some conversation and he left, test and recommendation in hand.

A week later he called to make an appointment. "I want to order that Danish hearing aid," he stated.

"Just yesterday men came to my door offering home hearing tests, and when they were finished they said, "There is really only one hearing aid on the market that would meet your need, and it is made in Denmark. We don't carry it, but that is what you should have."

He asked them to write it on their test, which they did, and he brought that in with him.

It revealed the same results as the test I had given him. I placed the order, which would take a couple of weeks to get.

In the meantime, they were curious about the differences in our beliefs. "What is the baptism in the Holy Spirit?" they inquired.

I read to them from a Bible I kept in my office, and because I was so busy with people waiting, I suggested they come over to our home some evening, which they did.

Appearing somewhat nervous and afraid, they sat in our living room, while we explained about the "enduing of power," which is for Christian service.

"God sent the Holy Spirit, just as Jesus promised," I said, "to equip the disciples for service. He did not send them out before that. Now they had what they needed: *Now they would be the equipment!*"

I told them that they had received the Holy Spirit when they committed their lives to Jesus Christ. Their vacant spirits had been opened to His Spirit, and He had come in.

"Now that same Spirit wants to come out!" I said.

"We let Him out by using our voices to give out those heavenly sounds and utterances," I informed them. "First, let's praise God and Jesus for the gift they want us to receive."

After a short time of praise and lifting our hands (they were very hesitant at first), they both began to utter those indistinguishable sounds the Spirit gives.

"I think it is just me!" Reverend Armstrong announced.

"It is you," we said. "God uses *your* mouth, *your* vocal chords and *your* lips. This is the miracle of God," we continued.

"Almighty God can energize you by His Spirit with your permission to speak out His mysteries."

They were both joyfully filled to overflowing with laughter and abandonment and said as they departed our home, "We will never be the same!"

I thought, *That's for sure!*

But ye shall receive power, after that the Holy Ghost is come upon you: and ye shall be witnesses unto me....

Acts 1:8

17

A Second Office

About one mile from our home in Minneapolis, I noticed a new office building with a sign outside that said, "Space for Rent."

When I inquired about this space, the front-door secretary pointed to eight doors of various cubicles and said that two were for rent.

Her job was to take all calls for the various renters, as there were no direct phone connections. The rent, by the month, was quite reasonable.

It seemed good to the Holy Ghost and to us, at least by the peaceful effect it had upon us. It was an ideal space, located at the intersection of two major bus lines.

I signed a month's lease and sent postcard notices to my Minneapolis clients announcing the additional location for their convenience, and the days and hours I would be there.

This office soon became too small, and I needed more room in Minneapolis. My four rooms plus reception area were fine in St. Paul, but there was no place for walk-in clients to sit down and wait.

I had been there only three months when I received a notice from the management that all tenants had thirty days to vacate, as the building had been sold.

I felt disappointed, because things were working out so well. Not knowing of any office space available, Phillip and I laid it out it before the Lord. We said we would look and knew He would open the space for us.

The next day Phillip reminded me of a building almost directly across the street that was "For Sale by Owner." I had seen it previously as I'd driven by to the supermarket, but I was not at all interested in buying a building—only renting.

One Saturday morning Phillip said he believed the "building" he was praying about might be the one for sale.

I agreed to look at it with him, on the condition that we would be able to rent it on some type of lease agreement.

As we walked over, we noticed the building was empty, but someone was inside. A nice young man invited us to inspect the one story and basement. I liked it!

It had a central hallway with two medium-sized offices on either side, one large room at the rear for a record/coffee room and parking spaces behind. It had a nice bathroom and a neat, clean basement.

Of course, I was *not* in the market to buy any building.

I suggested to the young man that he could do what the office building across the street did: rent spaces out, furnish a secretary and we would rent two or three spaces immediately.

"It is not my building," he stated. "My uncle is ill and in the hospital, and he only wants to sell."

"Well," I said very hesitantly, "what does he want for his building?"

"He won't take a penny less than what he paid for it!" was the swift reply.

"Yes?" I queried.

"Seventeen thousand dollars. That's it," was his answer.

Seventeen thousand dollars! That was probably the price he paid when he bought it twenty years ago! What a bargain, I thought.

Who wouldn't buy it and then resell it? It didn't take Phillip and me any time to tell him we would write him an earnest money check that day and go to our attorney and have the papers drawn up.

He had the legal description, tax statement and other documents, so we hightailed it to our attorney, got the papers ready and gave them to him that Friday afternoon.

We arranged to meet him at ten o'clock Monday morning.

I was mentally rearranging the spaces and reception area and placing furniture and equipment. What if he changed his mind? We could hardly wait for Monday morning.

A very sad face met us. The young man told us how sick his uncle had been, and unfortunately he had passed away Sunday evening.

The way he looked at us was so pitiful. But then he held out his hand to us and said, "My uncle signed your purchase agreement yesterday morning. The building has been cleaned, and we can close soon."

God Himself found that building and presented it to us! Not only that, but we had an agreement that we could occupy it immediately.

The probate took almost two years to settle the estate, and we occupied that building free, except for utility bills during that time, with only $1000 earnest money invested. We had new carpet installed and the decor updated, and we began with a flourishing business.

I thought we would never sell that building, but God had other plans we did not know about at that time.

We were being invited to various groups and churches, mainly evangelical, and God was beginning to launch us into ministry by His secret methods!

I know your [record of] works and what you are doing. See! I have set before you a door wide open which no one is able to shut....

Revelation 3:8 AMP

18

The Land *Purchase*

A month into my newly decorated office for the business I had taken over, an old gentleman called me.

"I've heard that you are Christians, and I would like to inquire about renting office space from you for my business."

I had a nice roomy reception area and four separate rooms, but I told him, "I don't care to rent out any of my space."

He went on, "I have been in ill health for some time, and my business has suffered from neglect. If you would reconsider and rent me a small room, I would come every morning at 7 o'clock to pray first for your business and then for mine."

I was touched by his demeanor and his confession, as a Nazarene, of a healthy relationship with our Savior.

Then I said, "You won't need to pay any rent. If you'll be here to pray for this business, we will be fortunate to have you here."

He was a pathetic-looking old man. Many times I took him to lunch and slipped money in his pocket.

I called his home when he had been absent from the office for a couple of days and found out that he was in the hospital.

Immediately we went to see him and went to buy him medicine, which his wife would not purchase. She believed in healing, but she didn't want to buy medicine.

We had healing prayers with him, and we comforted him with our love. He was back at the office in a few days.

Somehow I felt that this man, Ben, was God's provision for us. I was going to take good care of him.

Ben asked to come to our home one Saturday afternoon. He said, "I have a recurring dream about you and Phillip."

Phillip said, "Come over and tell us about it."

Ben said, "Both of you were standing with me on a high mountain bluff, overlooking a fertile valley. God spoke to me and said I would be gone, but you folks would own this entire valley. What do you make of that?"

We had no interpretation for his dream.

Later, Ben asked to come over again. He said, "I have met three doctors who make investments in property. They have a three-year option on a farm one mile east of Minnesota Mining. It has 120 acres, thirty of which are on the lake, and they want to sell it. If you will pay them the one-year equity they have in it, about $5000, you can acquire this farm."

I said, "Ben, we are not interested in farming." Phillip never said a word

I asked, "Ben, why do they want to sell if they have just learned the Minnesota Highway Department has changed the proposed route of I-94 to several miles south to connect with Wisconsin and not use Hudson Road?"

I also said, "Why in the world would we want to buy something that experienced investors don't want?" Again, Phillip was quiet.

My first reaction was negative. I wasn't interested!

The following Saturday Ben came over again. He went over the whole farm idea once more.

He told us the doctors were very anxious to sell for a reduced price, and he quoted a figure.

I shook my head and said, "We're not interested at any price."

Then Ben said, "Why don't you folks pray about it? I believe God wants you to buy it."

Now, it's one thing to hear directly from God, and it's another thing to have someone tell you they heard from God on your behalf.

Phillip said, "Let's pray that if the Lord would bless us with the amount supernaturally, we will buy the option."

I agreed.

We had built a small, unfinished cabin in Wisconsin several years earlier, but we had been too busy to use it for a couple of years.

So I put an advertisement in the paper, trying to attract a buyer. I only had one call, and that had been a year earlier.

I drove the one interested party eighty-five miles to see it. They liked it but admitted they only wanted to rent it for a two-week vacation. They had deceived me, so I'd given up on advertising it.

After our conversations with Ben, I decided to put another ad in the paper to sell the cabin. It was a small ad—no price listed, just our phone number.

I received at least twenty calls about it. I told every caller we'd be at the cabin the following Saturday and gave them directions on how to get there.

We were at the beginning of a dead-end lakeside frontage road that served eleven other cabins.

We went up early in the week to make sure everything was in order.

As we turned off, we noticed a large sign with all the cabin owners' names on this big stick. A new name had been added—"The Burkies."

Later in the afternoon, we decided to take a walk and locate the new Burkie place.

On our walk, the Holy Spirit would intercept our thoughts with many disconnected words.

For a few weeks prior to this day, as Phillip prayed, these words would come out in English: whiskey, Arctic Circle, Zenith radio, taverns, cement. Totally disconnected words!

It was a beautiful day. We noticed an older lady sitting in a lawn chair. Her husband was pouring her a cool drink.

"Hello," we said. "We're the Halversons. We're at the other end of the road."

We told them of our plans to sell our cabin, and then Mr. Burkie began to tell us all the work he had done over the past several months.

"All these guys you hire want to do is go to the taverns and drink whiskey," he said. "My cement work has been delayed because of their behavior."

We were alerted! He continued to rehearse the things in his life—about being in the Arctic Circle, where the only radio that worked was a Zenith radio.

Why would he tell us all this? It had nothing to do with welcoming them to the neighborhood!

Imagine what was going on in our spirits as we heard the very words the Holy Spirit had been speaking for several weeks.

It was an action time, and all we could think about was getting them acquainted with Jesus.

"Come down to our place in one hour and have supper with us," we said. They accepted. Our motive was to tell them about the Lord.

When they stepped into our cabin they loved it. They commented on the stairway going up to the loft and the field-stone fireplace.

We told them how we had bulldozed a big cliff eight years earlier and how Phillip and our son, Jim, had hand cut the beams to cross in the living room and kitchen.

At different times we'd bought close-out windows on sale and then made plans to fit them in. We'd built the cabin to suit the windows, but it had turned out well.

All of the lumber had been sawed by hand for the large beams. They had been lifted into place by block and tackle to make a big vaulted ceiling.

We told them all about the cabin, but we really wanted to talk about the eternal, because they were getting old. I knew that the Burkies, being good Catholics, feared going to hell.

Finally, we asked them, "Would you say today to Jesus, 'We accept You as our own Savior'?" They said they would.

Then we said to them, "You'll never have to worry about hell again. You are children of God, and you are going to heaven.

"If you pass away tomorrow, it doesn't matter if there's a priest to give you last rites. You've got the first rites of getting to heaven!"

Then Mr. Burkie asked, "Could we ask you the price you want for this cabin?"

We made up a price. He said, "If we'd only known, we would have bought this. We paid much more for ours, and it needs so much repair."

After repeating the sinner's prayer, they left our cabin with one of our Bibles.

The following Saturday was when all the people were coming to look at our cabin. People began coming when we were having breakfast at 7 A.M. We hurried to get dressed.

Since the time was set for 9 A.M., a line formed. We didn't let anyone in until 9 A.M..

Then a line of people walked in the living room and looked up at the loft.

The very first couple said, "We want to buy it. How much do you want for it? What do you want for a down payment? How soon can we close?"

I quoted them $2000 more than we'd quoted the Burkies. They said, "Sold! We'll take it. How soon can we occupy it?"

The cabin was sold by 9:30 A.M. All of the couples wanted to buy it. What a miracle!

We found out later that several of these couples had driven up to see the cabin before Saturday, and they had encountered the Burkies, who'd raved about our place.

The Holy Spirit engineered it, but they'd sold it for us before anyone came inside!

The next day Phillip said, "I suppose we had better call Ben." He wanted to tell Ben we had the money to make that option payment.

I said, "Oh, honey, let's just put the money in the bank and forget about the farm."

"Fern," Phillip said to me, "have you forgotten that we prayed and promised God if He would supernaturally provide the money for the option that we would go ahead with it?"

He looked at me with that Norwegian look that says, "I mean business!"

Then I had to admit my head was wrong but my heart was right.

This was God's intervention. It was supernatural.

We called Ben to arrange to buy this farm by Minnesota Mining, and arrangements were made for us to assume the balance of the farm option.

19

The *Highways*

In the meantime, as we prayed, other names and words would come forth by the Holy Spirit. "Jamison" was interspersed with other words. We didn't know anyone by that name. And at this time we had never heard of Vicki Jamison.

As property owners, we got a notice of a meeting to be held at City Hall on a certain date. We'd never been to any City Hall meetings, but we made plans to attend.

We were seated with about 100 other people in a large room. Two walls were covered with large maps.

The speaker for the evening was a Mr. Jamison. Because of this name coming in prayer, we were alerted to whatever he had to say.

Mr. Jamison was the new highway commissioner of our state, and the wall maps were a new configuration of the I-94 federal highway project—a major highway that goes through Minneapolis and St. Paul.

We learned that the Hudson road the farm was on was going to be upgraded significantly to eight lanes. The outer belt of the whole Minneapolis-St. Paul freeway would intersect with I-94 between our farm and the next farm.

We would be at the intersection of the only major free-ways on the east side of the Twin Cities!

Then the highway department contacted us and offered to pay us $80,000 if they could take part of our land to make part of the freeway on I-494 to cross. This was applied to the mortgage balance.

The new highway I-94 would take part of that and would pay us $80,000.

Some of our neighbors held out for more and were paid more, but we didn't. We thought it was miraculous.

We owned that farm for many years, and of course, the day after we'd bought it, I'd wanted to sell it. I just wanted to get rid of it.

Years later, we felt that we needed to sell. Phillip was talking about taking an early retirement, and we were going to begin the ministry. I had urged him for years to take an early retirement so we would have more time.

Suddenly a company from Chicago called, and the deal was completed. We sold the farm and got our money out of it.

When we sold the farm we paid tithes out of that money, and we paid for our house and a rental house. Then we gave all the rest of the money away.

We had enough money to live on, and that's all we needed. We didn't crave to have bigger houses and things.

Call unto me, and I will answer thee, and shew thee great and mighty things, which thou knowest not.

Jeremiah 33:3

20

Holman *Field*

After several trips to Brother Hagin's meetings held during that time at Sheridan Assembly in Tulsa, we received a phone call from Brother Hagin.

"I need to have a place for meetings in Minneapolis for about a week," he said. "Could you help me rent such a place, Phillip?"

"I will call you back to let you know what is available," responded Phillip.

We went to prayer right then. Getting up from his knees, Phillip felt impressed to call a minister of an old "River Lake Tabernacle" just across the Mississippi River from us.

The pastor, with whom we were well acquainted, was hearty in his welcome to Brother Hagin. "He can begin and end anytime he wishes, and we will accommodate him. We hope to have a few days to get the place shiny clean and everything in order. We will be honored to donate the facilities—no charges whatsoever!"

After a call to Brother Hagin, the date was set. Also, Brother Hagin asked us if we could accommodate a singer named Vicki at our home. Of course we could.

Eagerly looking forward to the continuing work of the Holy Spirit as we were being knit together with the Hagins, we picked them up at the International Airport between Minneapolis and St. Paul. We brought them to our home until a couple of hours later, when Phillip and Brother Hagin would pick up Vicki.

Off and on, Phillip had been praying the words "Holman" out of his spirit. But with the countless other things the Holy Spirit had been bringing forth, neither of us had connected it to anything. We learned not to, but to allow the Holy Spirit to make the connection.

The trip to the International Airport proved fruitless, as there was no incoming flight at that time from Dallas. Phillip then thought about "Holman Field"—a smaller airport in St. Paul.

Since Vicki would be coming in a private plane, Phillip suggested, "Let's head for Holman Field." Vicki was waiting there.

Vicki's singing added so much to Brother Hagin's meetings.

We said fond farewells to Vicki and Wes, her now deceased husband, never dreaming we would ever see them again, but a month or so later, we received a phone call from Vicki.

"We are flying down to Mexico City on business and some beach sunning, and we want to invite you to meet us in Dallas and fly with us, to be our guests for a wonderful time," Vicki said.

We were taken by surprise because this was the time we felt impressed to "show up in Sweden." What a challenge!

We were very honored to be invited but, at the same time, we knew we were to go to Sweden and had our clothes all ready, bags practically packed for the next week.

"Oh, Vicki," we said, "let us call you back after we pray about this because we have our clothes all packed for over-seas—Sweden."

"Don't worry," she responded, "you can buy summer clothes in Mexico."

Hanging up the phone, we looked at each other: "There is no way we can go to Mexico with the Jamisons," we both stated.

Our phone call to Vicki was met with regrets, but our hearts were settled.

We knew the Holy Spirit had spoken, and we had promised years earlier to obey God when we *knew* what we should do was revealed.

We ought to obey God rather than men.

Acts 5:29

21

Vicki

When we traveled with Vicki Jamison-Peterson, it was such a joyous time. (When Vicki remarried, she had added the name "Peterson" as her new married name.) Phillip had taken an early retirement from his government job, and we were free to go where the Holy Spirit led us.

We had such a big surprise when Vicki bought us a new Cadillac for traveling. We could all fit in it in between meetings at the various cities on the East Coast—Boston, Hartford, Springfield and others.

What a wonder to see the miraculous power of God at work when Vicki sang out the healings!

I still remember scenes like the hysterical woman who screamed out, "My goiter is gone!" while people seated near her tried to hush her for disturbing the service. Such scenes were the rule, not the exception.

Phillip led prayer services before the preaching services.

I recall a couple stopping us on the way into the main service and telling about the husband's loss of work and a need for a steady source of income.

We took the time right there to ask God for a steady job immediately for this man.

Then Phillip took some money out of his pocket and quickly put it into his hand.

Three weeks later, we received a letter through Vicki's office informing us of a miraculous job this man had received immediately. All we did was *ask* our Father.

Remember, Jesus Himself said, **If ye shall ask any thing in my name, I will do it** (John 14:14).

With the help of Vicki's office, we rented a tiny apartment close by her office for $350 a month.

As the time approached for us to return to Minnesota in the spring, we found ourselves wanting to buy a small house in Dallas rather than rent.

The realtor we called said she had just listed a house for sale for $26,000. She asked, "Would you like to be the first to see it?"

The minute we walked into that house we could see ourselves in it.

We admired the living room with fireplace and the adjoining dining room—both of which had ceiling-to-floor paned windows.

A large, five-window bedroom with its own full bath, and an equally large rear bedroom with its own bath, were separated by a small family room adjoining the kitchen and back hall, which was both an entry and the laundry area. The single garage was all we needed.

A doctor from Michigan had built it for his daughter, who was from Massachusetts, so the house had what I'd call "a Northern flavor."

I could picture us there for the winter months while we traveled with Vicki.

This bungalow was on the edge of a large Mexican community.

I thought I would learn Spanish just by listening to the families at the supermarkets—but they talked too fast!

The 4 percent mortgage made the payments $161 a month. We signed the papers to buy it.

Of course, we were anxious for October to come, packing some beds and linens in our trailer.

Vicki ironed and put up patterned sheets in one bedroom, and we located an eight-drawer dresser at the Salvation Army and a dining room set, which I still have.

Barb and Steve Arbo in Vicki's office were both from the north country of New England, and I was so pleased when they first entered our house and exclaimed, "A northern home!"

God richly blessed us with two wonderful neighbors who were Southern Baptists and who took pride in mowing our lawn when we were away during the summer months, as well as having a key in case of any emergency.

Eight years passed, and our comfy home was enjoyed by many friends, adding the warmth of fellowship.

We had planned to add screens to the back patio and a few other things, but God had a master plan we did not know anything about.

Suddenly Vicki announced that God was moving her to Tulsa!

We knew God had not directed us to Tulsa. I was "set for life" in our cute winter house in Dallas.

Because Vicki's ministry and travels were largely centered on the East Coast, she was led to begin a television ministry to that part of the country and tape it in Tulsa.

So when we were invited to be on her daily television program in Tulsa, Oklahoma, in August we drove from Minnesota to Tulsa expecting to come back to Minnesota at the end of the week.

After the first week's telecast, a large group gathered at Vicki's home, where we were guests. It seemed that every person there asked us the same question, "When are you going to move to Tulsa?"

We explained that we had no reason to move to Tulsa.

We had a very cute, comfy home that suited us in Dallas, and if anyone wanted us in Tulsa, it was only 250 miles, or an hour, to fly from Dallas, so why should we move? Besides, I didn't care much for Tulsa.

Later that night, as we prepared for bed, I related to Phillip what I'd finally told people: "If God wants us in Tulsa, all He has to do is rearrange the stars to spell out our names and we would surely move! Not until!" I had said it jokingly, so sure we would not move.

This was Friday night. The next morning we were packing our things for the trip back to Minnesota.

We drove to the dry-cleaners to pick up some clothes, worshipping the Lord as we went, speaking and singing in tongues to the Lord.

Suddenly the Holy Spirit spoke through Phillip, "You must move to Tulsa!" Then a pause, and again, "You must move to Tulsa!" Then quiet. The third time, slowly, "YOU... MUST... MOVE... TO... TULSA."

I said, "Phillip, we have to move to Tulsa. God wants us here."

When we arrived back at Vicki's, our news was met with cheers and dances of joy!

Having said our good-byes to Vicki, we left for Dallas Sunday afternoon instead of returning to Minnesota. As long as we were only 250 miles away, we would call a realtor and put our house up for sale.

That evening we visited with our neighbors, telling them we were moving to Tulsa and that our home would be for sale. In fact, we used their phone to call the realtor and leave a message on her answering machine to ask her to stop by and list our home for sale.

Monday morning we were in the backyard, raking up a few leaves and picking up a few pecans, when a woman came along the side driveway and said, "Mabel next door told me you want to sell your house."

"Yes," we said, "the realtor should be calling us soon."

"May I see your home?" she inquired.

"The door is open," I replied, "go ahead and look it over; open the closets and inspect it for yourself."

After about twenty minutes she came in the yard and said, "I am a bilingual teacher in the Dallas public schools and this is my district. For over three months I have been looking for a home, and every time I hear of one for sale, by the time I get there, it has been sold."

"I like your home, and I want to buy it."

Phillip told her we had owned it for eight years, and we wanted $86,000 for it.

Then he asked her, "What arrangements are you prepared to make, as we are planning to leave for Minnesota tomorrow?"

She replied, "My uncle died two years ago. I am his only living heir. The estate has been settled, and the money is sitting in the bank. You can have your money anytime you want it."

Within twenty-four hours after hearing from God that we were to move to Tulsa, our Dallas house was sold.

We thought of Habakkuk 1:5 AMP:

Look around [you, Habakkuk, replied the Lord] among the nations and see! And be astonished! Astounded! For I am putting into effect a work in your days [such] that you would not believe if it were told you.

We were astounded!

We were amazed!

22

Pastor *Rogers*

Phillip and I met with Vicki and Sharon, Vicki's pianist, in Vicki's motel room, where we waited on God and interceded for the services in Terre Haute, Indiana—especially for the evening service.

When Vicki had called our room that afternoon to come to pray, she'd said a Pastor Wayman Rogers from Louisville, Kentucky, would be there to pray with us about an urgent matter.

Before we went to prayer, Pastor Rogers told us of his large, growing church. "We have the largest Sunday school enrollment in the United States under the Assemblies of God denomination. We have them in every neighborhood all over town," he stated.

Their great need for more room had led them to a large tract of land near the intersection of two major highways.

Their finances were sufficient to begin the church building, and the congregation was full of anticipation for God to move in every way.

"However," Pastor Rogers continued, "an unexpected barrier has come up. To service the church with sewer and water, the local authorities have presented us with a big bill to cover the essential community services. It is an enormous amount of money, as this tract of land is next on the list for such improvements."

He bowed his head in his hands.

As we laid all this before the Lord, a great anointing came upon Phillip and he began to prophesy to Pastor Rogers: "In a short time the problem will be taken care of. Do not fret yourself over the matter—only worship and trust Me. I have provided."

This was given with such force and unction that we all gave a great big sigh of relief. *We knew the matter was already taken care of!*

Remember, *victories are first won in the Spirit!*

Pastor Rogers invited Vicki to come for meetings at the property. The date was open on her itinerary, and she accepted.

So later on, out in a field, the congregation assembled for the first outdoor meeting on their new property.

Vicki spoke from a flatbed truck, and the glory of the Lord fell upon us as Pastor Rogers told of God's financial miracle.

A huge apartment project was now going in next door, and the sewer and water lines had to cross over the grounds of the proposed church. As a result, *the church did not have to pay that huge amount of money! Heaven broke loose!*

Ahead of time, God was looking out for His own, using whomever He chose to convey His comfort and assurance and to minister to a need.

What do you think a crisis is for?

It is to focus your attention on what God has already provided for you.

If you have not been attentive to His precious Word, you have an excellent opportunity to *repent* and *refocus!*

You are **inaccessible in the secret place...** (Ps. 91:8 AMP).

23

A New *Nose*

Much prayer was made before we participated in Vicki's meetings. Like Brother Hagin says, "The Holy Spirit takes hold with us." Both before and during meetings, we gave ourselves to interceding for Vicki and the places we were scheduled to go.

"Intercession" means: INTER—coming between, like an *inter*city bridge connecting two cities, or an *inter*faith fellowship joining different faiths together for a purpose.[1] CESSION—the act of ceding, as by treaty, something as territory; transfer.[2]

When you *intercede,* you come in between God and people, as Moses did. You become a pipeline. What a privilege to be a part of God's operations!

As you keep your pipe clean, you will be blessed by the flow of His Spirit through you to others.

At another meeting in Louisville with Brother Rogers and his church, the auditorium was full and extra chairs were brought in.

As I was greeting people near the entrance, I noticed an older woman with a bloody bandage covering her nose. She held her hand over it. Some other ladies were with her.

As Vicki ministered to the needs of the people by singing out their healings, I fastened my eyes on the lady with the bloody bandage over her nose. She was standing with one hand raised to heaven and the other holding the bloody bandage.

Vicki left the platform, and we did too. When Vicki touched her, the bloody bandage *flew off.*

I jumped back, not wanting to be splattered with blood.

What I beheld took my breath away for an instant.

Before our eyes, a brand-new nose had begun to grow. We saw the cartilage and new skin forming, with no blood on her face!

Pandemonium broke out all around this woman and eventually throughout the entire congregation.

We later learned that cancer had eaten away her nose.

This was an instant creative miracle

Now unto him that is able to do exceeding abundantly above all that we ask or think, according to the power that worketh in us.

Ephesians 3:20

24

What Is Happening to

We were being summoned by the Holy Spirit to a town in Louisiana. Over and over the name "Gulf Shores" came with an urgency while we were praying and worshipping the Lord in our heavenly language.

"I want to invite you to come to my meeting in Gulf Shores," Vicki said on the phone the next day. "Can you join me on these dates?"

"Yes!" was our eager reply. "The Holy Spirit has already alerted us to be in that city."

This newly formed church was built like a pole barn and was filled with folding chairs to accommodate approximately 300 people.

Dramatic healings took place, which was normal for Vicki's meetings.

We were invited to have dinner the next noon at the pastor's residence. In the middle of our dinner, the pastor was summoned to the phone.

"I have lost my gold cigarette case," the woman stated, "and I have lost my desire to smoke!" She identified herself as Rosie.

The pastor assured her they would look for her cigarette case.

He also informed us privately that the woman had been a real trial to them because she was a Bible teacher in a Baptist church and was so opposed to "speaking with tongues."

She had spread word throughout the community that this church was "of the devil." Her advice to all was "Stay away from that church!"

On the fliers, Vicki was advertised as a singer who regularly appeared on the PTL program. People were urged to come to "hear this gospel singer."

On this particular night, Vicki called on Phillip to step forward and pray for the service. He did so.

Now the Holy Spirit "took hold," and with great urgency Phillip began speaking with tongues.

When the service was finally over, we were gathering up our things.

Down the center aisle marched a woman who had lost her cigarette case and reported it to the pastor. The pastor said, "Here comes Rosie."

She was angry!

She marched militantly right up to the raised platform and pointed her finger directly at Phillip.

"That's the man!" she cried. *"That's him!"*

"What is it you are so concerned about?" inquired both Phillip and the pastor.

She continued breathlessly, "While this man (pointing at Phillip) was speaking in that strange language, I heard the words in English. God was telling this city to repent and get right with God."

She continued with unbelief in her voice, "I know the devil doesn't want people to repent, and I know what I heard was God speaking to this city."

Rosie hesitantly stammered, "What is happening to me? I don't understand what is happening! I am upset because I was *tricked* into coming here," she said with anguish in her voice.

Phillip very gently invited her to join him and others who were already in the prayer room. He kept a watchful eye on her and encouraged her to worship Jesus, whom she certainly knew.

Phillip was standing beside her. He leaned forward to hear the most precious sounds of the Spirit of God gushing from her!

"Praise God, Sister," Phillip said to her. "That's right, God is filling you with the Holy Spirit. You are being baptized with His Spirit! Keep on now in that heavenly language."

She opened her eyes and in wonderment asked Phillip, "Am I speaking in tongues?"

"Yes, indeed!" was his instant reply. "Raise your hands again and keep worshipping your heavenly Father." She did!

Our last report of Rosie was that she had become a "flaming evangelist"!

It was God who maneuvered Rosie to that meeting for the purpose of transforming her Christian life to one of power and might.

> **Trust in the Lord with all thine heart; and lean not unto thine own understanding. In all thy ways acknowledge him, and he shall direct thy paths.**
>
> **Proverbs 3:5,6**

25

The Scandinavian *Trip*

Many people were going on a Full Gospel Businessmen's trip to Scandinavia. We thought about it, and friends asked us, "You're going, aren't you?"

We said, "We'll pray about it."

About five days before the deadline Phillip said, "The Lord wants us to go to Scandinavia." He said, "Wouldn't it be wonderful to go to Norway?" (He's Norwegian.)

I thought, *Wouldn't it be wonderful to go to Sweden?* (I'm Swedish.)

The Chicago Full Gospel office said we had to get passports. We got our passports in two days—the morning before we were to leave. I kept thinking we'd probably waited too long, but God was in it.

We had to get luggage and a wardrobe for the last part of April and the first part of May in northern Europe, which is cold during that season.

In Copenhagen two days later, Henry Carlson, the Full Gospel coordinator, asked Phillip where he would like to go.

Phillip said, "Norway," because he always wanted to be in the land of his heritage. Henry said he felt a strong impression to send us to central and southern Sweden. Phillip was happy.

For several weeks the Holy Spirit had been whispering to Phillip, *You will be sent. You will be sent.*

We had paid for our own tickets, but when FGBMFI says they're going to send you, they pay for everything, including hotels and meals.

It was a short plane hop from Copenhagen to Stockholm. I sat next to a soldier, and Phillip sat by the window.

The soldier mentioned the name of his country, and I said, "Oh, you're from behind the Iron Curtain."

He said, "Yes, we do not have the freedom you Americans enjoy."

I said, "You think Americans are free? They're bound with chains of sin and wickedness and do not experience real freedom and liberty until they meet Jesus Christ. Only then are they liberated from the guilt and penalty of sin."

We continued our discussion until we landed at Stockholm. He received our words graciously and thanked us for sharing with him, giving us a souvenir!

We found the train station to embark for our assigned area. We had to run since the train was about to leave the station.

When we arrived at a particular church, the minister was puzzled. We were scheduled for a different day according to his calendar.

As we were standing outside on the huge stone steps, a Saab automobile pulled up to an abrupt stop.

The woman driver informed us in quite good English that she'd been sent to pick us up and deliver us to another church some miles away.

When we got there, the meeting was in progress and it was dark. We could make out the tall white steeple and the beautiful stained-glass windows. The church was packed.

I'll never forget that first evening. The people seemed to surge with anticipation—first, because we were Americans.

Phillip had an interpreter because neither of us understood Swedish. I do a little bit, but I found out my grandmother's table prayer doesn't work when you want to use the bathroom!

Our interpreter, who taught at the local high school, spoke English very well. All the young people did too. Our interpreter and his wife were on furlough from Africa in mission work.

After the first meeting, Phillip said, "I didn't realize until the first meeting was over that when I lapsed into that heavenly language I was speaking Swedish."

I found out just before we left Sweden that I had prayed with the interpreter in his native Swedish language also. He told me I had related certain situations that concerned him and told him things that only he knew.

From the very first night, throngs of people came to the various locations throughout central and southern Sweden.

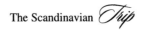

Our schedule for eight days was at least two meetings a day, often three, occasionally four.

We were in large high school classrooms conducting question-and-answer sessions, as well as giving our testimonies at radio stations and even at a large alcoholics' rehabilitation center.

> **In all thy ways acknowledge him, and he shall direct thy paths.**
>
> **Proverbs 3:6**

26

In a Swedish *Prison*

We were privileged to stay in the home of Reverend and Mrs. Stig Johannson in Sweden. They pastored five Baptist churches and were very close to Pentecostal churches. Neither he nor his wife, Beret, knew English.

The day Reverend Johannson tried to communicate to us that we'd be ministering at a prison, he didn't know the English word for "prison," so with fingers crossed over his face, he made himself look downcast and pulled at imaginary bars.

We studied his pencil drawing and with relief finally guessed, "A prison!"

Our interpreter explained that the prison at Coulough was the largest underground prison for hardened criminals in Sweden.

Since Reverend Johannson had not been able to arrange for any meetings there for years, he was delighted that the officials consented to admit the Americans.

The prison officials spoke to us in English and explained the security bell system. We were then led underground.

High skylights above us, we assembled in a room where approximately twenty psychiatric prisoners were. (We never planned on this, but God did.) I played the piano everywhere we went, and we sang a little.

As Phillip spoke through the interpreter, he told of an experience we had with a prisoner in the U.S. and of his dramatic deliverance from sin and his total commitment to follow Jesus.

To our right by the doorway as we were speaking stood three psychiatric doctors. In their white coats, they were observing us and the prisoners. I didn't know but what they might be expecting a disturbance or maybe they always were there when other people were around.

Suddenly, as Phillip was speaking, a tall, blond young man rose in the back of the room and marched right up to the front.

He stood directly in front of Phillip and said in good English, "I want Jesus to be my Savior."

Phillip excused himself and this man to a room across the hall, where he was directed to go.

As Phillip was finishing praying with this man, a prison guard appeared and said, "Please come quickly."

A middle-aged man in the front row where we had been speaking had created quite a disturbance. The demons within him were speaking in a high-pitched voice: "I ruined your meeting."

Two guards were trying to control him. No one knew what to do.

As Phillip quickly observed the situation and breathed the name of Jesus, he perceived that this man was demon-possessed. So he put his hands on each side of his head, and the Holy Spirit actively joined in prayer.

In a loud voice, Phillip commanded the demons to leave "in Jesus' name."

The demons cried out, "Don't say that name! Spell it, but don't say it!"

In the continued, forceful use of the name of Jesus and utterances in tongues, Phillip commanded all demons, "Depart!"

"We know we have to go, but we have no place. Where shall we go?" they asked.

Phillip consigned them to an uninhabited desert part of the earth.

The man slumped down in his chair like a wet noodle. He was not an English-speaking person; but demons can speak in any language, and they did so that day.

We knew this man wasn't completely delivered, but the prison's first warning bell had rung and we had seven minutes to get out before the gates automatically locked us in for the night.

The three psychiatric doctors wanted to talk to us in the hall. They said they wanted us to minister all throughout the prison to well-guarded small groups.

They said they had heard that Pentecostals had power like this, but they had never seen it.

We would have liked to stay and spend the whole trip there, but this was just prior to Phillip's retirement. He still had a job to get back to even though God was already working in us a desire to let go of the job and be where He needed us.

Firm plans for the remaining days in Sweden had been made with Full Gospel Businessmen's Fellowship, and it was not up to us to change them. We had to follow the plan we had committed to.

At that time, within my spirit—and Phillip said the same thing—was a great longing to return to that prison **to preach deliverance to the captives...** (Luke 4:18).

27

A *Reunion*

Before we left for Sweden, a man of limited experience in God came up to Phillip in our little church in Minnesota. He told Phillip that he'd had a vision of Phillip and me in Sweden.

He said, "I saw you preaching, and I saw an old man asking for prayer."

Then he said, "In a separate vision, Fern was sitting up in the balcony of a large church playing the piano."

The first fulfillment of the prophecy occurred when I was unexpectedly called upon to provide the piano accompaniment for a singer in the church.

We were in a traditional Lutheran church, and the Lord had told Phillip something that he was to speak on that night.

When Phillip was speaking, he paused and was interrupted by a voice from the back of the church.

An older man with white hair stood up. In a sobbing voice, he asked if Phillip would please pray for his son, who hadn't been heard from in many years. He wanted to be able to see his son once more before he went to be with the Lord.

A _Reunion_

The whole congregation was moved by his anguish over his son.

Remembering the prophecy we had been given, the Holy Spirit took hold in power, and we recognized another mark of confirmation on our ministry.

We prayed and believed that the son would return and this man would be reunited with his son.

I remember the word that came forth: "Soon!"

In a couple of days we were back in Stockholm and some people met us on the street and hailed us down.

They said, "We enjoyed hearing you." Then they said, "Do you remember the last service we were in when that old man came forth?

"The very next day the son unexpectedly returned home to his father.

"The father went to all the neighbors with his son on his arm, telling them, 'Look, my son is back.'"

Isn't that wonderful?

And they went forth, and preached every where, the Lord working with them, and confirming the word with signs following.

Mark 16:20

28

Unexpected Swedish *Youth*

Sweden is remarkable for its grandeur. In fact, all of Europe is noted for its magnificent old buildings.

In Sweden they have state churches—huge cathedrals with high ceilings, ornate marble altars and splendid chandeliers that grace the buildings. Yet these buildings are used only once a week—on Sunday mornings—for eight or ten old folks.

The majority of the young Swedes don't exhibit any interest in "religion."

We had been told of this lethargy in all of Scandinavia, so we were stirred from the first meeting to find that about 50 percent of our attendees were young people. A full church!

The young people followed us everywhere. If there weren't enough seats, they sat on the floor in the aisles or directly in front of the altar.

In this gorgeous Lutheran state church we were in, we enjoyed a grand tour before the meeting began.

The grandeur of this particular church is a marvelous memory.

On each side of a long path from the church's front door were the monuments of the departed faithful pastors.

Most of these churches had the graveyard right in front, so you walked through a path where there were gravestones of departed church members.

This was to be our very last meeting in Sweden, and young folks were there by the score.

When Phillip finished speaking he had some occasional utterances in tongues. He wasn't sure how to proceed, so he paused quietly to pray and invited the audience to join in prayer.

As he finished his prayer he heard a moving about. You never know what you're praying when you pray in tongues.

Young people surged to the altar, weeping. They climbed over the altar rail (which they're not supposed to do), and they went into the reserved inner sanctum.

Phillip didn't know what he said in tongues, but all heaven broke loose in that magnificent church!

Not only did many receive salvation, but as the Swedish workers talked to them, many were filled with the Holy Spirit and began to speak with other tongues.

It was a noisy time in such a formal state church!

Phillip was shaking from head to toe. He would almost lurch as if to lose his balance. He was drunk in the Spirit.

When he had finished praying, he took a little time with a certain young man. The interpreter later informed him that he was a student who was a toughie and an incorrigible. Here he was weeping in repentance before the Lord.

Later, we were informed by letter of his life change that continued to be confirmed in this move of the Spirit of God among these youth.

God broke through. He does what no man can do. When they see it, the pastors want it too.

> Not in the way of eye-service [as if they were watching you] and only to please men, but as servants (slaves) of Christ, doing the will of God heartily and with your whole soul;
>
> Rendering services readily with goodwill, as to the Lord and not to men.

Ephesians 6:6,7 AMP

29

An Oslo *Mission*

We only had one day left before the entire FGBMFI airlift that had disbanded to various European countries was to meet in Stockholm.

Phillip had prayed much about Oslo for several days, and we thought as long as we had one free day we'd take a train over to Oslo just for the day, then go back to Stockholm.

We believed God had a purpose for us in Oslo, and I was glad Phillip could set foot in Norway and get that Norwegian soil under his feet.

God did have a purpose for us there.

The passengers on the train kept to themselves.

Scandinavians do that. They seem to be aloof, but they respect your privacy—not as a snobbish thing but as respect.

We found everyone to be very hospitable, opening up if we spoke to them.

An elegantly dressed lady right across the aisle from us offered to share some fresh fruit when she knew we were Americans.

When we disembarked from the train, we inquired about a place to buy the famous Norwegian wool sweaters. We strolled along and finally made our purchase.

Phillip and I bought matching sweaters, and we also bought one for our son.

Since we had eaten on the train, we weren't in the mood for a meal, but we decided we'd have a sandwich in the park adjacent to the shopping area.

We purchased some picture postcards, mostly to impress people back in the States, you know!

We were addressing them and wondering where we could find a postbox to get some stamps.

I noticed a tall, blond young man across the park coming in our direction with books under his arm.

I said, "Pardon me." (You speak loudly and slowly because you think they can understand better.) "Can you tell us where we can mail these postcards?"

A long, high-pitched voice resonated without speech. I said, "In the name of Jesus, speak."

Immediately he pointed and said in perfect English, "There's a postbox around the next corner over there."

Phillip asked, "Do you live here?"

Again, "Ohhhh," until we commanded him to speak in Jesus' name.

Every remark we made, he responded with this high-pitched sound until the name that's higher than any name was spoken.

He informed us that he was a student on his way to a class at a university near the park, and he was studying comparative religions!

We knew we were in the right place at the right time! Those were demons to prevent us from continuing with him. We took authority, and we put the heel on Satan's head!

He told us he wanted to study to find out who the true God was.

We told him about Jesus and His claims on his life.

He said he was going to be late for his class so he was anxious to be on his way.

We didn't wish to detain him, but we said, "When you confess Jesus as your Lord and Savior, you will be free from your speech impediment."

We never saw him again. But he knows in his spirit when he confesses Jesus as Savior, he will no longer have a speech impediment.

Mission accomplished!

There were many train stops on our way back from Oslo to Stockholm. I had asked about a berth so we could sleep on the train, but it was full.

However, a lady suddenly changed her plans and got off. Since she had paid full fare to Stockholm, Phillip and I were given her berth free of charge.

The Father had us specifically in mind to see to our comfort!

We slept with our clothes on. The Holy Spirit surrounded us, and we felt absolutely abandoned to His love and care.

We returned home from this trip with a stronger commitment to serve God with our full strength and be utterly dependent on the Holy Spirit.

At the name of Jesus every knee should bow, of things in heaven, and things in earth, and things under the earth.

Philippians 2:10

The Spirit intercedes and pleads [before God] in behalf of the saints according to and in harmony with God's will.

Romans 8:27 AMP

30

Donald Oman, *Live!*

Often Phillip prayed during the night. Usually I would awaken because it would be so loud, but I would drift in and out of prayer.

One night I heard Phillip praying a particular name, which he did often, but this name was different: *Donald Oman.*

Several times Phillip prayed in a very authoritative voice for the intervention of the Holy Spirit.

Then, in a decisive, loud command he spoke these words: "Donald Oman, in the name of Jesus Christ, stand up. Live, in the name of Jesus. Live! Live to finish the work I have for you to do."

A holy awe filled our bedroom as we both realized the Holy Spirit was active on behalf of someone named Donald Oman, whom we did not know.

A few months passed, and we were visiting a church we had formerly attended. We were astonished to see the name "Donald Oman" on a prayer request list distributed prior to the meeting.

After the meeting we inquired of the person who had compiled the prayer list, "Who is Donald Oman?"

The person said, "His mother-in-law is here this morning."

We found her and told her about the outstanding prayer we had experienced in the Spirit.

She told us her son-in-law, Donald Oman, was a missionary in Lebanon in charge of an orphanage with his wife.

He had been ill and struggled between life and death at times. Finally, he succumbed and efforts to revive him were fruitless.

Because of the custom and the climate of the country, plans were made for his immediate cremation.

To prepare the body for cremation, they bind it up with wood, twigs and twine to carry it to a fire.

As they were preparing him, his wife cried out, "O God, spare Don! Please, God, spare my husband."

At that precise moment, his wife said, "Visible signs of life began to manifest in his body."

He was released from the bondage of the wood, twigs and twine, and he came forth weak but alive.

When she told us the time this happened, we ascertained that it was the same time Phillip was interceding in the Spirit, even precise with time zone differences.

Donald Oman came back to the United States and regained his health. He lived many years and finished the work the Lord had ordained for him.

Phillip and Fern Halverson, Married August 24, 1940

Vicki Jamison-Peterson interviewing Phillip for radio and television (1977)

Jim Kaseman, Billye Brim, Phillip Halverson (1981)

Phillip and Fern in Norway (1983)

Phillip and Fern teaching on prayer at one of Kenneth Copeland's conventions (1983)

Jim and Kathi Kaseman, Branson, Missouri (1999)

Linda Gassler, Monticello, Minnesota (2000)

Lynne Hammond (2000)

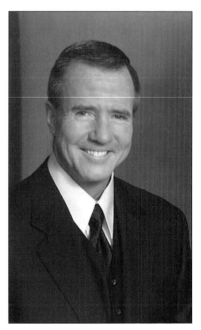

Mac Hammond (2000)

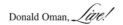

He preached for thirteen more years and built a church, and we had the privilege of preaching in this church.

Obviously, it was God's will for Donald Oman to be raised up to complete his work!

> **Likewise the Spirit also helpeth our infirmities: for we know not what we should pray for as we ought: but the Spirit itself [Himself] maketh intercession for us with groanings which cannot be uttered.**
>
> **Romans 8:26**

31

At About *Dusk*

Phillip and I were part of a prayer group that met regularly, not only to pray for individual requests, but also to rejoice over the answers to prayer that we had experienced.

We met in different homes every two weeks, sometimes in our home.

The group was made up of people who loved to pray and intercede with groanings and travail until the peace of God replaced the particular concern. We shared each other's concerns in united prayer.

One particular evening in 1964, having been in prayer earnestly for a couple of hours, Phillip issued these English words very loudly: "At about dusk. At about dusk."

The Holy Spirit went on to describe a terrible shaking and devastating destruction, naming many cities in Alaska.

The fifteen or twenty of us who were assembled that night will never forget it.

Early the next morning, I received many phone calls. The first caller asked, "Have you seen the morning paper?"

I said, "We don't take the paper."

The person said, "There has been a great earthquake in Alaska that occurred at the same time we were praying last night."

The newspaper article began with the very words that Phillip had spoken out: "At about dusk."

The word of knowledge was in operation at the prayer meeting. Some might ask, "What good did it do? It didn't prevent the earthquake."

It revealed that Phillip was a man of God and that the Holy Spirit was speaking through him. George was a part of this group.

This became a way of life for both of us.

He [the Holy Spirit] will announce and declare to you the things that are to come [that will happen in the future].

John 16:13 AMP

32

Business Venture *Warning*

George, a fairly new Christian who had been filled with the Holy Spirit, was present with his wife as we prayed.

We were thrilled to see the gifts of the Spirit operating in his life so early.

We had been saved for years, but George and his wife had just started coming with us to meetings.

George was considering the association of himself with some men in business. He had even come to our home asking for prayer regarding some of the business plans.

Both Phillip and I had prayed with George several times. By the Holy Spirit Phillip was given a strong impression that this man was *not* to go into this business.

Phillip agonized so much for George in prayer that he called him and begged him not to get involved in this proposed business venture.

One day I had such a tremendous burden, I couldn't get my work done. Our advice and tears for George had brought no action.

George was at the prayer meeting on that Good Friday night.

God had established Phillip's credibility with a true word that night and at other times with George, but he chose to go into this business endeavor only to fail.

It was spiritually draining and not God's will for him. Ultimately, he experienced a big financial setback. Many Christian friends of George lost thousands of dollars.

Neither Phillip nor I ever prayed to ascertain God's will for anyone. But if God burdened either of us in a definite area, we contacted the people involved and informed them of the concern of the Holy Spirit.

> **Therefore be always alert and on your guard, being mindful that for three years I never stopped night or day seriously to admonish and advise and exhort you one by one with tears.**
>
> **Acts 20:31** AMP

Chapter 33

Censored

These words came in prayer as Phillip was praying: "Censored. Censored. Censored."

One day a letter arrived, and stamped across the face of it was the word in big, bold, black letters, "Censored."

A spiritual alert sounded! It was a letter from a prison inmate, and he requested contact with us.

If we wanted to make contact with him, we were to acknowledge it on an enclosed card and return it to the prison officials.

Jack had been in Phillip's Sunday school class many years before, and he had also been in mine.

His whole family was saved. The family had moved to New York to begin a new business and had not found the Christian fellowship they'd needed so desperately. We'd lost all contact with them for many years.

Jack had a brilliant mind and it had gotten him into too much trouble. Eventually his career in crime had landed him behind bars.

As he had sought to end his life, he'd managed to slash his wrists, only to live with guilt and despair.

He said that one day when he'd been in solitary confinement, agony had overwhelmed him and he'd cried out in desperation, "Oh, God, send someone to help me. Help me, God!" God had heard his cries.

Our faces had appeared to him, and through prison officials he'd contacted us.

We wrote him and told him how honored we were to be counted as his friends. And not only were we touched with his story, but we wanted him to know we would do everything we could to be a strength to him and stand by him and his family.

We assured him of our prayers and of the Holy Spirit's intercession for him.

He was encouraged, although still desperately depressed.

His wife, Joyce, was pressing for a divorce. His letters to her were returned unopened.

One day I stopped by their apartment, and Joyce answered the door. She told me, "He writes me, but I don't even open the letters. I return them unopened."

Of course, this caused Jack great torment. He was sick from thinking about losing his wife and young son.

His furniture and his car were repossessed because of nonpayment.

We knew we had a part to play and that God would deliver.

The letters poured back and forth between us. Every day I would sit down at the typewriter and God would give me Scriptures and encouraging words for Jack.

One evening Phillip and I decided to stop and meet Joyce and their four-year-old son, Greg.

Joyce was bitter against her husband. We asked if we could help, and we also asked her if she had a Bible.

We told her that when her husband was a boy he had accepted Jesus as his Savior.

She abruptly left the room. We were surprised when she returned with a Bible.

We presented Christ as the only answer. When we asked if she would accept Jesus, she said she couldn't pray but she would repeat a prayer after me.

Then a surprising turn! She called her son and said, "Greggie, you pray like Mommy did." So we prayed with him, and he repeated a prayer too.

We urged her to read the book of John first and then added that we wanted to keep track of her by stopping in or calling.

We gave her our phone number, and we had her and Greg in our home for meals and sometimes overnight on weekends.

As we left, I was tempted to think she'd just repeated the prayer to be polite. The animosity she felt for her husband gave me the impression that the Word of God had not been sown in good ground.

However, I was determined to nourish that ground so it could bear fruit. I knew it was God's will for me to do that.

One afternoon I stopped for coffee with a couple of sweet rolls. I chatted with her, read Scripture and asked her if she would please reconsider her attitude toward her husband.

When I asked her about her Bible reading, she said, "Well, yeah, I read it, but I don't get anything out of it."

I told her what John 8:31-32 says: **If ye continue in my word, then are ye my disciples indeed; and ye shall know the truth, and the truth shall make you free.**

I explained to her that the first way to obey the Lord was to show love.

I said, "I wonder, Joyce, how can you show God you really want to obey Him and partake of this freedom? I know you have had it tough, but your husband has had it a lot tougher. Why not send him a note?"

No response. I headed home.

While I was preparing our evening meal for guests, the phone rang. It was the first phone call I had ever received from Joyce.

She said, "I just came from the drugstore, and I mailed a short note to Jack."

That's when I knew Joyce had the spark of God living within her. She had deliberately determined to obey what I'd told her.

I was more determined than ever to fan that spark. Phillip continued to pray much in the Spirit about "censored, censored."

One night we took Joyce and Greg to an ice show. Another night as we were dropping them off after a special concert at our church, Phillip handed Joyce some money privately.

The next day I was close by Joyce's apartment, so I stopped to say "Hi."

She had been to a hairdresser and had the fanciest hairdo, complete with several hairpieces. My first thought was, *Joyce, you and I are going to have to have a little talk about the value of money.* But it wouldn't come out.

Instead I said, "Joyce, you look beautiful. Your hair is gorgeous."

I was glad I hadn't let the old flesh come out and scolded her as I'd wanted to.

This was the beginning of a real change in her relationship, not only with us, but with her husband.

During the next few months, communication opened up between Joyce and Jack.

His letters to us were full of praise and expectancy about his future, which he had totally committed to the Lord. He'd become a student in Kenneth Hagin's correspondence course.

Jack said, "Even in prison, I'm a free man."

Jack's appearance changed dramatically from nails that were bitten down to the quick, bloodshot eyes and nervous motions, to a very self-confident, eager-to-learn, eager-to-please and well-groomed young man.

Three natural facts existed, but remember, the supernatural always exceeds the natural:

The parole board reviewed his record and said they would not allow a parole.

His family lawyers couldn't get anyone to budge for a parole.

His long sentence appeared to have no chance of ever being shortened.

Phillip and I interceded for Jack and held him before the Father as if he were our own son.

I was startled when Phillip prayed these English words: *"The prison bars are broken at Christmas."* Often while we were in prayer, these same words would come out.

At that time, Jack was the only person we knew who was in prison. We had been to the prison often—not to see Jack, because he was allowed only two visits a month. We simply wanted him to be with Joyce and with his family.

We were invited by the chaplain to conduct some early Sunday morning services and to substitute for him occasionally when he would be out of town, which we did.

The night before Christmas Eve we went to Joyce's parents' home, where she and Greg were spending the holidays. We took a gift of a pretty nightie and slippers to encourage Joyce to hope for a second honeymoon.

We were startled by a knock at the door. Her father opened the door, and there stood Jack grinning from ear to ear.

We felt like Rhoda when Peter was released from prison by the angel. We couldn't believe our eyes!

Jack was out on a work-release program, and he never entered prison again. The prison bars were broken at Christmas! A word of wisdom!

Today Jack and Joyce have a beautiful home and furnishings, a car and a boat. He is a respected member of his community.

For a number of years, we received a beautiful floral gift every month, no matter where we were.

And for several years in Minnesota, every time we had a big snowfall, our driveway would be completely cleared by this outstanding young man before we ever got up.

What a joy and a treasure he has been to us!

We then that are strong ought to bear the infirmities of the weak, and not to please ourselves.

Romans 15:1

Chapter 34

Meeting Jim *Kaseman*

It was just a couple of weeks before Christmas. We went to the Broken Arrow, Oklahoma post office to mail some packages.

Every once in a while we would hear the names *Jim Kaseman* and *Billye Brim*. We had met Billye, but not Jim Kaseman.

A long line had formed at the post office, and we slowly moved forward. I was very aware of an old man directly in front of me. He had such a worried look on his face, and he was trembling.

He turned in my direction, and thinking he might be saying something to me, I said, "Are you getting ready for Christmas?"

He said, "Christmas? Everything's gone wrong today, and I don't care to hear about Christmas."

Touching his coat, I said, "What has happened to you today?" Phillip was right behind me.

He began a litany of troubles. His roof had leaked in three places overnight. His cat had gotten out, and he couldn't find it. His electricity had been shut off.

I began to comfort him in sharing that he could have a new beginning right then.

He said, "Is that right?"

I said, "Yes, Jesus said it, so it must be true."

I was talking loudly enough that the people around could hear me plainly.

I said, "Why live the old life when you can have Jesus' life in you?"

This man consented to repeating a prayer after me and then thanked me.

The man ahead of him turned around and looked at us. He had on a big fur hat like Minnesotans wear.

He said, "You really move right in, don't you?"

We introduced ourselves. He said, "My name is Jim Kaseman."

I said, "Are you the Jim Kaseman who works for Billye Brim?" (Billye Brim worked for him at the time, but I didn't know!)

He said, "Well, you might put it that way."

Since this time, we have been together many times to pray with Jim and Kathy Kaseman and with Billye Brim—and we've loved every minute of our times together!

Behold, I will do a new thing; now it shall spring forth....

Isaiah 43:19

Chapter 35

Quick *Check*

One morning as Phillip and I were praying in tongues for Jim Kaseman, the English words "quick check" kept coming out.

At the time, Jim was traveling to Iron Curtain countries to deliver medical supplies and to "smuggle" in Bibles that were printed in the language of the people.

It was illegal to take Bibles into these countries, so it took a lot of faith to walk out what the Holy Ghost was directing.

At the border of one of these countries, Jim was prevented from crossing over because the guard said his visa was not complete.

Sometimes people would be detained for days or even weeks for this reason.

Jim prayed to get through customs, and back home at the same time we were praying that God would prosper his journey.

When we finished praying I said, "Phillip, we've got to call the Kasemans to have Kathy tell Jim when he calls that the Spirit is praying 'quick check.'"

Kathy called us back within two or three hours and said, "I just talked to Jim, and he said the papers were not ready yet. They were being detained because their visas were not in order."

Jim agreed, "That's it. Quick check. Everything in this trip is going to be quick. We're going through three countries— quick check, quick check, quick check." Jim's trucks were then allowed through customs.

Just as their visas were being checked again, a lady came down the steps from another building with an enormous bouquet of flowers.

She came to Jim's truck and said, "Congratulations!" Theirs was a certain number truck going through customs, so the flowers were a reward!

She said, "Go on your trip and have a wonderful time."

When Jim got back from that trip, he said, "There has never been a trip like it." Every place he went, everything was in order.

After the message, "quick check," Jim said, "The guards hardly looked at our visas and waved us through. We were able to distribute all of those medical supplies and to meet with underground Christians to distribute all of the Bibles."

Blessed is he that considereth the poor: the Lord will deliver him in time of trouble.

Psalm 41:1

Chapter 36

Rhema *Students*

We made the move to Tulsa. Except for a bed and a few linens at our home in St. Paul, furniture was finally in place. We were very happy.

I loved the breakfast room off of the kitchen, where we would linger over coffee and survey the climbing apricot-colored roses on the patio.

It was everything I could ever want in a home. We had three bedrooms, one of which became an office. Then we had a guest bedroom and bath and a huge master bedroom with bath, all with large walk-in wardrobe closets.

We put our house in St. Paul on the market by placing a "For Sale by Owner" sign on the front lawn. On one side was our telephone number in St. Paul for when we would be there, and on the other side was our son Jim's phone number. We would just turn the sign around as we came or left.

Remember, at this time we had always gone south for the winter around the first of October, and we would be back north around the first of May.

We felt we were to have something to do with Rhema students in the midst of our travels, but we weren't going to do anything to bring it about. The Lord would have to make the necessary arrangements, and we would be obedient.

After all, we don't know *anything* except the Spirit of the Lord reveal it, which is revelation knowledge.

We have *learned* a lot through books, teachers, schools, universities and experiences. When the teacher in school gives you a test, you are supposed to put down the answer that is deemed "correct" according to someone's book or opinion.

It is said that we now live in "the information and knowledge age." Great insight into the natural and scientific realms has been made.

But that has nothing to do with supernatural knowledge! Only the Holy Spirit can transmit the supernatural.

You were born again into the *supernatural,* or *spiritual, realm.* Your life didn't change from the day before you accepted Jesus as your own Savior. But you were given a new spirit. Now you have two within you—your spirit and the Holy Spirit.

You can let the natural spirit guide you as you did before—and we do need to have information to function in life for planning meals, figuring income taxes, driving a car and so forth. These are all learned experiences and behavior.

The Holy Spirit of God imparts *real* knowledge. The Bible defines knowledge as *knowing.* Genesis 4:1 says, **And Adam knew Eve his wife; and she conceived, and bare Cain....**

God's impartation comes from intimate fellowship with Him.

A heart full of thanksgiving and praise, with a desire to communicate His goodness and mercy to everyone, is the prerequisite.

Your mind will often oppose the Holy Spirit. That's why Paul says, **Let this mind be in you, which was also in Christ Jesus** (Phil. 2:5).

It is up to us to decide which spirit we want to dominate us.

We were approached by Berith Heinnonen, a pastor from Finland who had just enrolled for the two-year course at Rhema Bible Training Center.

We had met Berith two years earlier in Finland where we ministered in several of her churches, under the direction of Jim Kaseman.

Rhema classes had already started, and Berith had a request: "Some of us students are having a prayer meeting Friday night, and I wonder—if you are in town, would you come to speak to us and pray with us?"

"Yes!" Phillip said immediately. "We will be in town, and we will be glad to be with you."

A larger than planned number of students—about fifty—crowded into a large home that night, sitting mostly on the floor close together. They gave us their rapt attention.

We shared about the dynamic work of the Holy Spirit in our lives, how we had embarked on this amazing adventure with Him. It was a good meeting.

After we got to our home from this prayer meeting, Phillip and I had such a deep sense of exhilaration in the Spirit.

Phillip said, "Fern, I believe this is why we have come to Tulsa. If Berith invites us to come next Friday night again, we will tell her we believe we are to be with these students *every* Friday night and we will arrange our schedule of meetings accordingly."

Two days later, after the Sunday evening service at Rhema, Berith came to us and said, "All the students and others who heard of our Friday night meeting want to know if you would come again this Friday night. Will you be in town?"

"Yes, we will, Berith," Phillip replied, "because the Lord has directed us to not only come this Friday, but every Friday night during this school year to teach students about the work of the Holy Spirit and prayer."

The next Friday night, and from then on, we had over 100 students jammed into whatever house we met in, eager to learn more about the moving of the Holy Spirit—to enable them to minister effectively when they left Rhema and went out into the world where God would place them.

We told them we knew we were to be with them, and only Rhema students would be admitted. We would arrange our schedule to fit every Friday night, since that was the purpose of our move to Tulsa.

I can remember flying out to California to fulfill meeting schedules for the following week and then flying back to Tulsa on Friday—only to leave again on Saturday to go back to California (or wherever) in order to be obedient to God's direction to us.

"A mark of our ministry among you," Phillip said, "will be a confirmation of our teaching so you will see the results for yourselves."

That very night we were in Dennis and LeAnn Krey's house, and one of the prayer requests was from them.

They needed to sell or lease a Kansas farm they owned in order to have enough money to support themselves and two children while at Rhema. Several people had seen the farm, but none of them had offered to make a transaction.

Just as our prayer session was coming to a close, the telephone rang. LeAnn answered it and came back into the room to announce that a couple who had previously looked at the farm called to ascertain the price and terms.

Needless to say, God handled the whole farm transaction for them.

This was a confirmation for the Rhema students of our prayer teaching!

And there were others. Two come to mind.

The urgency of a phone call in this house brought us all quickly to a place of prayer. The lady who called was distraught.

She screamed, "Lee, my son, is writhing in agony on the floor! It must be a kidney stone," she ascertained from the location of the pain.

"Pray with me now that this pain will cease!" she demanded.

Immediately the Holy Spirit "took hold with us" (as Brother Hagin often says).

Suddenly she said, "Hold on...." The phone was quiet.

We kept waiting.

She came back to the phone, almost panting and out of breath, to tell us her twenty-three-year-old son had "just passed a fairly good-sized kidney stone!"

"I have it in my hand," she screamed. "God has delivered Lee from all the pain. Thank you," she said.

Her first reaction to evil was to pray and get someone to agree.

That should always be our priority. Then the Holy Spirit has the opportunity to show His power.

The Rhema students were given innumerable examples of the Holy Spirit at work during this year.

With Thanksgiving break approaching, many prayer requests were made for various needs.

One young lady was concerned about going to her widowed father's home. He was an unbeliever who lived alone and had resented her and her young son's conversions.

Earnest prayer was made on behalf of all the requests, and the Holy Spirit "took hold."

Returning from the Thanksgiving holiday, we heard an amazing testimony from this young lady.

Rita had prepared a turkey, dressing and all the usual accompaniments for a show of love to her father. She went to a lot of work to make sure the dinner would be special for the three of them.

As they sat down at the table, she asked her father, "Is it all right, Dad, to ask God to bless this food?"

"Okay," was his abrupt reply.

But her seven-year-old son interrupted quickly, "Mom, can I please say a Scripture I learned?"

"What is it?" she inquired, glancing at her father.

For God so loved the world, that he gave his only begotten Son, that whosoever believeth in him should not perish, but have everlasting life (John 3:16), he recited.

Rita had bowed her head, but when she looked up, she saw tears streaming down her father's weathered cheeks.

"God loves you, Dad," she said, leaning toward him.

As she simply explained the forgiveness of sins by Jesus to him, the tears continued to flow.

Thanksgiving Day became a new birthday for her dad!

What an unusual circumstance!

How innovative the Holy Spirit is!

He knows!

We don't know anything!

37

It's Only a *Picture*

At Kenneth Copeland's 1983 convention in Anaheim, Phillip and I were again honored to be invited to teach on the Holy Spirit and prayer.

During one of his evening services, as Brother Copeland was concluding his message, I heard my name called from a distance: "Fern. Fern. Fern."

As the voice grew louder I opened my eyes to find Brother Copeland prophesying to me. Among other things, he said, "The Lord will be visiting you with dreams and visions."

When we returned to our home in Tulsa, the first night I had a dream of Brother Copeland.

The next night I had a dream of Gloria Copeland, and we said we would relay these dreams to them in the next convention in Charlotte, North Carolina.

Later that year, as Phillip and I were ministering in California, we were traveling to a meeting with a pastor and his wife.

Pointing out some of the well-known sites, we were told that the building we were in front of was Universal's studio for indoor filming.

Shortly after returning home, I had a dream of that particular Universal Studio building in Burbank and was taken inside, where there was a wide staircase and a long balcony.

It began to unfold to me by revelation of the Holy Spirit in my sleep. The staircase could be used for weddings and the beautiful bride would make her entrance, complete with trailing veil and an awaiting assemblage of guests.

However, the building had other scenarios. I saw a barroom brawl erupt into a gun battle, and bodies were falling over the balcony with blood dripping from them.

The Holy Spirit explained that films were made in that studio. Months later, the film would be distributed to a network of theaters all across the country and people would pay hard-earned money to sit and watch the barroom scene.

It became so gruesome that some people had to look away from the scenes or cover their eyes to avoid seeing the horrible spectacle. It was too gory!

Now, the Holy Spirit emphasized, other people in the theater would remind the nauseated ones, "Remember, it's only a picture!"

As I awakened, those words, "It's only a picture," continued to fill my spirit and my mind.

As I prayed about this vivid dream, I understood this is exactly what Satan does.

A co-worker comes to you and says, "I hear half of us are being let go."

A doctor gives you a bad medical report.

You learn that your spouse has been laid off.

Word reaches you that friends have lied about you.

Fear grips you. Satan is waving his banner in front of you to get your attention. Immediately, you begin to think of the consequences. You cannot get your mind off of this turn of events.

Your spirit is troubled.

You cannot find peace.

The churning in your stomach gets worse.

No food agrees with you.

The grip of fear has you as paralyzed as a fly in a spider's web.

It's only a picture!

Satan confronts you with reports constantly. I had an opportunity to prove this in a most unusual, bizarre way.

The following winter, as we were praying together, I heard myself say, "Show up in Sweden."

I said to Phillip, "We need to pray for someone to show up in Sweden."

The very next day as we were meditating on the Word of God, again the Holy Spirit spoke through me, saying, "I want you to show up in Sweden."

You will guard him and keep him in perfect and constant peace whose mind [both its inclination and its character] is stayed on You, because he commits himself to You, leans on You, and hopes confidently in you.

Isaiah 26:3 AMP

38

Not *True!*

We had our tickets, and everything was set for us to leave on Friday for Sweden.

Thursday morning the phone rang and the voice said, "Mrs. Halverson?"

I said, "Yes."

The person said, "This is Metropolitan Medical Center. We have your daughter here. She's been in a car accident. We can't reach anyone at her home."

I said, "She is my daughter-in-law." I knew my son was out of town, but he would be back sometime that evening.

I said, "We'll be right down." We went to the emergency room, praying all the way there. "God, keep Kris, our darling daughter-in-law. Keep her safe in Your hand."

When we arrived at the emergency room, no one paid any attention to us. There was no one there to take our names or see what we wanted.

Finally, we asked a nurse about Kris.

She said, "If she's in the emergency room, she hasn't been released yet."

Finally a doctor came out and said, "The emergency room waiting area is on the second floor."

In this waiting room people were reading newspapers, smoking cigarettes, talking about someone not going to make it, planning funerals. The devil had them all whipped!

A man came in the room and called out our names. We stepped out in the corridor with him. He was the nicest looking doctor, the kind who seems as though you could trust with anything.

He said, "I'm Doctor so-and-so. Kris is on her way to a room."

We asked, "What has happened to her?"

He said, "She was in a car accident, and we have not been able to bring her around yet."

He was bracing us with the thought that she might spend the rest of her life in a wheelchair. They try to pave the way, so when the crash comes, you expect it!

That's exactly what Satan wants to do. He wants you to accept what someone is saying to you, but you must expect what God is saying to you!

While the doctor was talking to us, in my spirit came up, "Liar! Liar! Liar!" This was not a man you'd call a liar. But what he was saying was a lie. I knew it, and Phillip knew it.

I turned to Phillip and said, "It is only a picture, and it's not true!"

Not *True!*

The minute the doctor was about to go, he said, "Follow me."

We went down the corridor with him into a room, and there was Kris lying in bed. She had long, beautiful hair and usually wore it up or back. It was down, covering part of her face.

The doctor leaned down to Kris's ear and said really loudly, "Kris! Someone is here to see you. Kris!"

She turned her head and looked at us through her hair with those big eyes.

She said, "Oh, it's Mom and Dad."

The doctor looked totally amazed.

We hugged and kissed her.

We said, "Kris, you're just fine."

She said, "I'm fine."

We said, "You're just fine. We know it."

Even when you're in a comatose or semi-conscious state, what is spoken registers in your spirit.

On the way home we stopped by their home. Jim was just going from his car to the house.

We told him, "Kris is in the hospital, but she is fine. They want to keep her overnight.

Jim went to the hospital and stayed with her. The next morning he checked her out of the hospital against the doctor's orders.

Kris has since testified in some of my own meetings in California how she's never had a moment of pain. She has been just fine, and she is a display of health all the time.

God was right there. Don't look at the natural pictures, such as keeping someone in a wheelchair. It's only a picture!

Look at what God has spoken to you. Quote the Word!

Then watch Him perform it when you have steadfast trust in Him!

I am alert and active, watching over My word to perform it.

Jeremiah 1:12 AMP

39

Show Up in *Sweden*

One morning Phillip spoke out in English while he was praying in tongues, *"Show up in Sweden."*

I wondered, *Lord, how can we show up in Sweden? We don't have an invitation.*

He spoke to us several times, *Show up in Sweden.*

Phillip said, "We'll just trust God to make a way. What we need to do is call Scandinavian Airlines in Minneapolis, and we'll call the Norwegian travel service."

We called and asked, "What openings do you have for traveling to Stockholm?"

The woman we dealt with said, "Send me a check for $300, and I'll put your name on a list in case there's an opening. You can have first choice at it. I have no one else on the list."

We got it ready and put it in the mailbox.

The same day, we received a letter from a black church in California where we had ministered.

They said, "We were praying for you, and God directed us to send you this check." The check was for $350.

Phillip said, "Already God has given us more back in the same day than we sent to the travel office."

In about a week the lady from Scandinavian Airlines called and said, "I have an opening on this date for you to go to Stockholm, but it's first class."

We said, "We'll take it."

It was pretty expensive, and we never kept extra money. Phillip had his pension from early retirement from his government job, and we had enough money to get along on.

We weren't out to make money or to hoard it upon ourselves. We gave most of our offerings away.

We planned to land in Sweden and wait there at the airport because all we knew was that we were to "show up."

Mama Goodwin had called us to go with her to some meetings in Houston in the interim. (Brother Goodwin had departed to be with the Lord.)

The meetings were wonderful. During the last meeting, we were on the platform, shaking hands with the pastor and his wife, and getting ready to go back to our hotel.

A couple came up the aisle right toward us. They said to my husband, "The Lord spoke to us two weeks ago that we were to put a check in an envelope and He would show us where we were to give it."

They handed the envelope to Phillip, and he handed it to the pastor because we never took money from church members.

They weren't church members there, however. They had never been to this church before. So the pastor handed it right back to us. He said, "I wouldn't touch it."

This couple said, "When we came in the auditorium tonight, God showed us that we were to give it to the man who was speaking." (Phillip was speaking.)

We opened the envelope in front of everyone, and it was a check for $10,000.

We blessed those people and asked the Lord to give them back double in return.

The next day we left in the morning to return home. There was more than enough money to pay for the first-class airfare. El Shaddai!

Phillip said, "Let's take this money with us when we show up in Sweden."

In the back of my mind I was thinking, *We're probably going to need that money.* But God had a lot of other plans for it.

Both Jim Kaseman and Billye Brim knew we were going to "show up in Sweden."

Jim said, "That's the very time we're going to be at an island right outside of Stockholm. We'll get the word out that you're going to be there."

So there we were with our pockets loaded with money, which we converted to tens and twenties and put in different envelopes in our luggage.

This was our first trip to Sweden. The people from Lapland (who sold reindeer to make a living) had sold some of their things so they could come by train to our prayer meetings. Our interpreter said, "They don't even have much money to buy food here."

We knew we were the supply source. Jim Kaseman's word got out fast. We taught and spoke about prayer.

We distributed all of that money, except enough to pay for our fare. I think we saved approximately $1,500 of it for ourselves. The rest we were able to give away to the Laplanders.

God had a plan for us to simply show up. All you have to do is just show up and you'll be at the right place at the right time. Be ready to be a pipeline!

Be instant in season, out of season....

2 Timothy 4:2

40

Denver's First Pastors'

Prayer Conference

We were invited and indeed honored to be speakers with another minister at the first Denver Pastors' Prayer Conference.

There were only three days left of that year, and we were due back in Tulsa to be on a New Year's Eve television show with Vicki Jamison-Peterson.

A lady singer and her husband and small baby were also on the platform to be introduced. She had a beautiful voice, and everyone enjoyed her talent.

The last night it was our turn to minister.

When the worship leader asked the singer to come, she refused to leave her seat.

We knew she had received bad news that afternoon about her mother's worsening condition in her bout with cancer. This information depressed the lady so much that she could not minister in song.

However, since it was our service, Phillip came to the podium and began to pray in the Spirit. After an interval, Phillip walked over to this dejected young woman.

He took her hand, and she arose and immediately fell over his extended arm like a wet noodle.

Still praying, Phillip continued to hold her up over his extended arm.

Suddenly she went into a trance—straight and stiff, eyes wide open—and laid on the platform. Both of us knelt at her side.

I gave a signal to her husband in the front row to come up to the platform. He took his place near her.

A mighty and powerful demonstration of the Holy Spirit took place. Phillip quaked and shook, speaking in the Spirit. This continued for some time.

As she lay on the platform, with her husband kneeling by her side, Phillip came over to the podium, drunk in the Spirit, eyes closed, and then went over past the young lady, down about four or five steps to the audience level. I sat down on the steps.

He not only spoke in the Spirit, but he also spoke in English, weaving about like a drunk and dancing a jig.

What a first prayer conference for these pastors!

We left the next noon for Tulsa.

About three weeks later I answered the phone, and it was this singer. It had taken her this long to get our unlisted number.

The very night I have just described—when she refused to sing, having received the evil report about her mother— something happened.

This is what she told me.

First she shared, "When my husband and I talked with you when we first met you in Denver, we had already decided to separate. We thought we had better keep the commitment to the meeting and then call it quits. Our marriage was over!"

I was stunned to hear this.

Then she shared that while she was in a trance on that platform, her father was driving her mother on what he expected to be her final trip to a hospital in Louisiana.

As they were driving, her mother, lying in the backseat, stated that she wanted her husband to stop at a restaurant.

A restaurant! She hadn't eaten much of anything for so long and had no appetite. He saw a restaurant and pulled in.

Not only was she hungry, but she ate a full barbecue meal and *was completely well!*

She continued, "I have been trying to get your phone number, and no one would give it to me until now."

She asked me what size I was. When I told her, she said she was sending me a beautiful new mink coat!

I protested, telling her that I didn't need a fur coat, living in the South.

"That's all right," she said. "God told me to send you this fur coat, and I will obey Him!"

The woman was ecstatic in relating the bizarre way God does things!

Their marriage was saved and prospered!

Her dear mother was miraculously healed!

Joy and laughter filled them!

And I have had the opportunity to hear that rich voice since in meetings!

> **Then shall we know, if we follow on to know the Lord: his going forth is prepared as the morning; and he shall come unto us....**
>
> **Hosea 6:3**

41

Billy's *Departure*

Billye Brim's first church in Collinsville, Oklahoma, used to be a tire shop. She kept a sign in front of the building that said, "We fix flats!"

The building wasn't very large. It couldn't have held more than 100 chairs. There was a tiny raised platform in one corner that held the electric organ and the podium.

It had a good-sized parking area.

We were honored to minister, either alone or with Billye, many times. The Oklahoma people were very easy to get acquainted with, and we enjoyed the fellowship.

Billye traveled a lot, and she selected Reverend Lee Morgans to pastor The Glorious Church of Collinsville.

Getting acquainted with Pastor Morgans and his wife was marked by the power of the Lord displayed and glory surrounding all of us. The wonderful atmosphere reminded me of 1 Kings 8:11:

The priests could not stand to minister because of the cloud: for the glory of the Lord had filled the house of the Lord.

One day as Phillip was in prayer, he said to me, "I have to call Billye right away."

When I heard the next words, "God is going to call Billye home, and I have to reach her now," I caught my breath, not wanting to believe such a thing.

Phillip called and talked to Billye several times that day and inquired of her whereabouts. Where was she going? How long were the next meetings and when? How was she feeling?

Billye was full of enthusiasm as usual and, I'm sure, wondered why Phillip had called her, because he didn't say much.

The Holy Spirit continued to give advanced notice about Billye's departure.

I remember two other occasions when those very words would manifest in prayer and within a short time we would learn of the person's death.

Phillip was quite agitated about this prayer.

We prayed on behalf of Billye and her work, lifting her up for strength.

The next day our phone rang. It was Billye: "Oh, Phillip and Fern, please pray for Pastor Lee Morgans—his father passed away suddenly and unexpectedly today. We are all devastated. Lee was so close to his father, Billy."

"Was his father's name Billy?" inquired Phillip.

"Yes, and please come with us to Lee's side to comfort him."

Now our understanding was opened. Now we realized the timing of God in gathering this precious man to Himself.

We had never met or heard of Lee's father, because he'd attended a different church.

But what a comfort to know a call had been made by the Holy Spirit and we were witnesses to His sudden and majestic doings.

We joined in mourning with Lee and Jan Morgans at the celebration, which Pastor Lee conducted for his father.

> **Surely the Lord God will do nothing, but he revealeth his secret unto his servants the prophets.**
>
> **Amos 3:7**

42

Company's *Coming*

Phillip and I had gone on a diet to do without sweets.

The Lord said to me, "Company's coming!" So I made a huge cake.

The aroma brought Phillip in from the garage.

He had a big smile on his face, and he asked, "Is coffee ready?"

He saw the cake. I assured him we were not going to eat any of it. He looked at it longingly.

No company came to our house that Saturday evening.

The following morning I felt strongly that we should take the cake with us to church.

We were going to minister at Billye Brim's church that morning since she was out of town.

I got a knife and some paper napkins from someone and decided to cut the cake and serve it to the congregation.

A couple in their early thirties came into the church with their two children—a son about four and a baby about six months. An older gentleman was with them too.

They were very poorly dressed for such a cold day.

They had lost their farm in Kansas, so they were on their way to relatives in Arizona when their truck broke down right in front of the church.

Pastor Morgans brought them into his warm study and led them to the Lord.

They had no money. Even the baby had no stockings on. Their tennis shoes were worn out.

A couple of men from the church were able to fix their car.

Pastor Morgans introduced the newly born-again family just as I was serving the cake.

We took up a substantial offering for them and gave them the rest of the cake as well as some clothes that were on hand.

All of the congregation stood up and said, "Company came!"

That's when it dawned on me: This was a celebration I didn't even know about. God sent these people. They were our company!

For I was hungry and you gave Me food, I was thirsty and you gave Me something to drink, I was a stranger and you brought Me together with yourselves... I was naked and you clothed Me....

Matthew 25:35,36 AMP

43

The Hearse Without a Corpse

One day Phillip was putting the finishing touches of polish on his car while awaiting the arrival of his brother and his wife, Brad and Jean.

In their morning phone call, they said they would only have time for a quick cup of coffee.

The coffee was perking and the light lunch was ready when they arrived.

Brad and Phillip talked in the garage while Jean and I set the table.

Jean shared with me her concern for a friend, Mrs. Edwards, who had suddenly become ill.

Mrs. Edwards' husband, the local mortician, had rushed her to the small local hospital.

There was nothing they could do for her, so she was transferred to a larger hospital about fifty miles away.

That hospital, in turn, recommended she be taken immediately to Mayo Clinic, where they diagnosed her condition as an inoperable brain aneurysm.

When the doctor informed Mr. Edwards about the hopelessness of his wife's condition, he also told him that the hospital would call to tell him when he could pick up her body.

It was a very sad Mr. Edwards who had shared this with Jean and Brad. Jean told me to be sure to pray for both Mr. and Mrs. Edwards.

We called the men in for lunch. After the quick visit, we bade them Godspeed on their return trip.

After a full day, we went to bed, and I had completely forgotten that I had promised Jean that we would pray for Mrs. Edwards. I had not said a word to Phillip about it.

That night Phillip's mighty prayer awakened me. He was forcefully uttering in the Holy Spirit in tongues: "Intervene for Mrs. Edwards! Intervene for the aneurysm!"

Over and over again the Holy Spirit spoke these words.

When that subsided, I said, "Phillip, that must be for the Mrs. Edwards Jean was talking about today."

"What Mrs. Edwards?" Phillip asked. "Who is Mrs. Edwards? What about her?"

"Didn't Brad tell you about the mortician's wife?"

"No. What about her?"

Then I related that brief history Jean had given me, and we continued to pray for Mrs. Edwards with our natural understanding, commanding the aneurysm to be dissolved and her whole body to be made perfectly whole in Jesus' name.

We prayed that she would be instantly whole with no effects whatsoever from this encounter. We prayed fervently for perhaps half an hour, interceding for Mrs. Edwards with thanksgiving and praise for her deliverance.

Two days later, Brad called and said, "Phillip, I have to tell you what happened to our friend, Mrs. Edwards.

"Yesterday, Mayo Clinic called Mr. Edwards and told him he should come and pick up his wife.

"He drove the hearse to Rochester, planning to pick up her body.

"As he entered the large lobby, he thought he saw a vision to his left.

"He was met by his ecstatic wife, who didn't know anything about her former condition except what the doctors had told her when she was discharged."

Phillip then told Brad about the astonishing experience that we'd had in prayer two nights before.

The Holy Spirit had mightily intervened.

Phillip and I were so amazed that the following weekend we drove to visit Mr. and Mrs. Edwards to verify this tremendous miracle.

I am alert and active, watching over My word to perform it.

Jeremiah 1:12 AMP

44

Justin

It was a cold February day in Tulsa. In our morning worship time with the Lord, the Spirit of God took hold with us.

A "Justin" was being called forth by the Spirit, as that name occurred several times during prayer. We did not know a single person by the name of "Justin."

Early that afternoon we went to get groceries at the Safeway store.

When we were checking out, Phillip and I headed out to the parking lot with two large bags of groceries.

"Did you notice the young couple behind us?" I asked.

"I only noticed their cute baby," Phillip replied.

"Phillip," I said, "they only bought a quart of milk and a loaf of bread."

I continued, "They are in trouble."

We headed right back to the store. This young, slender man and his pretty Filipino wife with the baby had just checked out and had moved to a counter to put a blanket around the baby.

As we approached them, Phillip put his hand out to shake hands with the young man. There were not many people in the store, and there were no clerks near us.

"Pardon me," Phillip said, "I was just wondering if you had a job."

The young man looked slightly puzzled. "Did you see me using food stamps?" he asked.

"No," replied Phillip. "I only noticed your baby." And with that, Phillip pulled out a bill from his back pocket and stuck it in this young man's hand. "I'd like for you to have this."

"Well, this is highly unusual," said the young man. "I have had a few odd jobs since moving here in August, but I have not been able to get steady work."

He opened up his hand to uncover the twenty-dollar bill.

When Phillip saw the surprised look on his face, he said, "I'd like to do something for you. I'd like to pray for you that God would give you a good job."

Still surprised, the young man murmured, "If it pleases you."

"It pleases me," said Phillip. And taking his hand, Phillip said a short prayer and asked our Father to "give this young man a better job than he could hope for."

Then I proceeded to get their names and phone number, wanting to make further contact with them.

The next day was Saturday. My repeated efforts to reach them to invite them to Rhema Church were intercepted by the operator, who said I had either dialed incorrectly or else that number was no longer in use.

"Oh! I know what happened," I said to Phillip. "They didn't want us to know their phone was disconnected because they probably couldn't pay the phone bill."

We determined that on Monday we would call the phone company to find out the amount owed so we could pay it and be able to reach them.

When I was assisted by another operator in the billing department, she told me it was a working number. "Did you dial 1 first?" she inquired.

I hadn't thought of Owasso as a suburb of Tulsa. When I dialed correctly, the young wife answered the phone.

I reminded her who we were and asked if my husband could speak to her husband.

"He just went for another job interview," she responded.

Then I asked her to have her husband call my husband when he returned.

At 6:30 that evening the young man called and asked to talk to Mr. Halverson.

"Mr. Halverson!" he exclaimed. "I went for a job interview this morning, and the company said I had all the qualifications they were seeking. They put me to work at a permanent job, better than I could ever have hoped for!"

After a brief conversation, we invited them to our home, and Phillip commented on their cute baby.

"What is your baby's name?" he inquired.

"Justin," they replied, never knowing how the Holy Spirit just zeroed in on what He wanted to do that day!

We were touched by their *need!* Don't be *miracle-conscious! Be need-conscious!* Then God will turn the situation into a miracle!

> **Finally, be ye all of one mind, having compassion one of another, love as brethren, be pitiful, be courteous.**
>
> **1 Peter 3:8**

45

Little *Stevie*

Barbara Arbo, a well-known minister of the Word, worked for Vicki Jamison Ministries in Dallas.

She met her future husband, Steve, at Vicki's office.

Phillip and I became acquainted with both of them as we spent that first winter in Dallas, which became our winter home for eight years.

I remember how Barbara and Steve wanted to have a child. "Sarah is to be her name," they announced.

Much later, one morning at breakfast Phillip told me he'd had an unusual experience as he was awakening.

"It was like a vision of Steve Arbo," he related, "except he was so tiny." (Steve Arbo is a big man.) Phillip could only describe what he saw as "Little Stevie."

That very afternoon the doorbell rang. There stood an excited Barb and Steve.

Over coffee they shared their exciting news with us: Barb was pregnant! They wanted us to pray for little "Sarah."

Phillip hesitated, and then he told them of his morning experience and about "Little Stevie."

We noticed Barb's face fall.

"But," she cried, "I'm believing God for a little girl."

We prayed and asked the Lord to bless this child in her womb and to put His mark of anointing on the baby all the days of its life.

Little Stevie was born about seven months later!

Howbeit when he, the Spirit of truth, is come, he will guide you into all truth: for he shall not speak of himself; but whatsoever he shall hear, that shall he speak: and he will shew you things to come.

John 16:13

46

Surprise *Baby*

"Uncle Phillip, please pray for me," said the caller, one of Phillip's nieces. "I have not been well and finally decided to see a doctor as my stomach is swollen."

The anguish in her voice expressed her fear.

"Karen, you have done the right thing by asking for agreement in prayer," responded Phillip. "Tell me about your trip to the doctor."

"After a thorough examination and every kind of test you can think of, he told me I had a growing tumor and would need an operation," she said.

The frustration in Karen's message was evident. She knew she was not pregnant, since she still had her monthly period.

"Tell me," continued Phillip, "how is your baby Emily?"

"She is walking on her own now and into everything!" Karen happily related. "She loves to have me read to her, especially the account of Samson and his enormous strength."

As Karen related these family things, she seemed to be more like herself.

"Let's pray, Karen," said Phillip. "The Lord's strength is measured by our obedience and confidence in His ability."

The power of the Holy Spirit came upon Phillip in a marked way as he prayed. I joined in on the other phone.

"Father, I thank You that You have given us the power over all the power of the enemy. Karen and I agree that this tumor will wither and die, in Jesus' mighty name. Full health and strength are restored to Karen *now* and distress ceases. Joy and gladness in the midst of this condition are hers *now!*"

And then a pronouncement: "Karen, you are going to give birth to a healthy baby girl!" The force of this statement took the three of us by surprise!

Three weeks later, little Joy arrived—six and one-half pounds of healthy, kicking flesh!

> **Do not be afraid...for you have found grace (free, spontaneous, absolute favor and loving-kindness) with God...**
>
> **Luke 1:30 AMP**

> **For with God nothing is ever impossible and no word from God shall be without power or impossible of fulfillment.**
>
> **Luke 1:37 AMP**

47

I'm Not As Old As I *Look!*

The lines were long on this bright Saturday as we stood outside the bank.

I was casually listening to a conversation behind me among three older ladies. They were talking about their crafts and ideas.

"I'll never live long enough to do or finish all the ideas I have," exclaimed one of them. "You know, I'm not as old as I look!"

My spiritual ears heard this too, and I turned around, smiled at these lively ladies and decided to participate in their exchange.

"Do you have any idea how long you'll live?" I asked.

All three shook their heads and murmured, "No."

Then one woman repeated her statement, "I know I'll never live long enough to do all my ideas."

"Life is so uncertain, isn't it?" I asked. Continuing, I offered, "If you should live only one day more, what would you choose to do?"

Each one had a thoughtful answer: Finish a baby quilt for a grandchild...stencil the kitchen table...use the knitting yarn for mittens for next year's Christmas gifts.

"But," I said, "if you only had the one day, you wouldn't be around for Christmas." They murmured something to agree.

"But on the other hand, suppose you all lived to be 100 years old and your time came to die, and you knew it. What would you do?" I queried.

The answers varied: "Just die," said one. "Hope for the best," another answered. "I'd be so scared of dying that I'd hate to think about it," said the third woman.

I had a wonderful opportunity outside in that bright sunshine to explain how the guilt of sin weighed heavily, and that Jesus—whom they had all heard of—took that guilt and rescued us from the penalty we feel as humans.

I had the honor and distinct privilege of having these three ladies repeat the prayer of salvation. I got their names and addresses and sent them each a gospel of John with my telephone number.

One called me back tearfully to tell me she appreciated my remarks and since then felt peace.

If thou shalt confess with thy mouth the Lord Jesus, and shalt believe in thine heart that God hath raised him from the dead, thou shalt be saved. For with the heart man believeth unto righteousness; and with the mouth confession is made unto salvation.

Romans 10:9,10

48

Move! Hide! *Duck!*

Phillip's nephew and his new bride called to ask to come to Minneapolis to have prayer with us regarding his imminent call by the military to Vietnam.

It was a hot day, and as we sat in our backyard, the earnestness of this couple, in the face of the unknown, touched our hearts.

They did the right thing: They asked for agreement in prayer for safety in the midst of battle.

The Holy Spirit took hold with us, and Phillip rebuked Satan's power over Eddie and gave the angels charge over him.

The couple departed with gladness and a certainty that God was surely in charge of them and would return Eddie safely to resume their newly married life.

In the two years that followed, the Holy Spirit would interrupt our prayers or just speak out as we were meditating or reading Scripture:

"Duck behind that tree now!"

"Lie down right where you are!"

"Move three feet to your left!"

"Hide in that depression on your right."

These were all loud commands. Neither one of us understood what they meant, but obviously they were commands for someone in danger.

We didn't make any connection with Eddie. It was only when he returned and we learned of his experience that we put it together.

"Uncle Phillip," he said, "enemy fire was so loud and constant with my buddies dropping all around me, but I would hear loud, clear instructions of what I was to do. I definitely knew where to turn, where to duck or hide, or which protective measures to take. I know God was protecting me. There is no doubt about it."

Then Phillip told him of our experiences while Eddie had been in Vietnam.

We rejoiced together over the loving care of our Father for one of His own who had placed his trust completely in His almighty hands!

We all sat in wonderment of how God uses people to bring about His promises.

Recently, we joined them in the celebration of their twenty-fifth wedding anniversary.

It was just as Shadrach, Meshach and Abednego had said:

Our God whom we serve is able to deliver us from the burning fiery furnace....

Daniel 3:17

A fourth man got in the furnace with them and **upon** [their] **bodies the fire had no power, nor was an hair of their head singed, neither were their coats changed, nor the smell of fire had passed on them** (Dan. 3:27).

49

A New Baby—*Cody*

Phillip heard the Holy Spirit say the word "Cody," among other things, while in prayer, and he thought it might be about Cody, Wyoming, where he and others had hunted.

Regularly in prayer or worship, the word "Cody" would be spoken.

Long before this, and of course unknown to us, a baby named Cody had been born to a couple in California.

Neglected by his parents and lying in his own fecal matter, the welfare department placed the infant in foster care. Later, Cody was given up for adoption.

Little Cody had been so deprived that he didn't respond to a human voice. Workers determined that he was severely brain deficient. He looked like a tiny, limp, wizened old man.

There was a childless Christian couple who wanted to adopt.

They made supplication to the Lord daily, but their chance of being in line for an adoptive child at any time in the near future was remote.

They felt the Lord would have them take a handicapped child to rear, and that's what led them to Cody's social worker.

Once the paperwork was completed, they took this pathetic, helpless child into their loving arms and tended to him as if he were a prince to some throne!

Holding and cuddling him, they faithfully read the Bible to him, although they had no assurance that he could even hear.

They spoke love to the little one who had only known rejection.

They sang songs of Jesus and His love to him and played tapes of healing Scriptures and songs in his room.

Their believing prayers ascended to the Father, along with the love they expressed to him.

Cody remained in this condition, not gaining weight for a month while in their home.

But suddenly and dramatically everything changed!

Cody began to eat vigorously, moving his limbs forcefully. His face filled out, and those little brown eyes now studied his new mother intently.

He smiled frequently and began to make sounds. They noticed how eagerly he responded to sounds and the bright colors of the nursery.

I can't trust my memory for accurate details on the rest of Cody's development, but just a few years ago we were told Cody was a perfectly developed toddler with no trace of brain impairment or of his deplorable beginnings.

You see, the Holy Spirit "took hold" as Phillip prayed, agreeing with the desire of that couple's hearts of love and compassion.

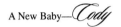

The Word the parents spoke over the child brought *life* and *health* to baby Cody!

Behold, I am the Lord, the God of all flesh: is there any thing too hard for me?

Jeremiah 32:27

50

Ivar

One day I was impressed to go to the local veterans' hospital to pray for my father's friend, Ivar, who was in a coma and who was not saved as far as we knew.

Phillip had been praying in the Holy Spirit for an "Ivar," so when I said, "Phillip, could we go out to pray for Ivar?" he quickly agreed.

The nurse on duty on Ivar's floor told us he had been comatose for two weeks, hadn't had any visitors and was unresponsive. Then she left to perform her other duties.

We were just outside Ivar's door, so we tiptoed in. He was alone, sleeping in a six-bed room. He looked ashen—dead.

Leaning over his bed, I touched Ivar's shoulder.

"Ivar, we have come to talk to you and pray with you."

Ivar's eyes opened suddenly and met mine.

Softly, I said, "Ivar, we have come to tell you God loves you and He gave Jesus to be your Savior. Do you know who I am?"

"Yes! You are Rudy's daughter, Fern," said an alert Ivar.

We were startled! We were witnessing a miracle!

Phillip gently took Ivar's hand and prayed, "Father, reveal Jesus to Ivar now as Your blood cleanses him from every sin and he becomes Your child."

We hadn't taken more than two or three steps toward the door when we heard his voice and turned to see him raised up on one elbow.

We returned to his bed to hear him say slowly, "Th-thanks a lot, th-thanks a lot, folks." We were awed.

Those were his last words. He went to be with his Savior that night.

Hebrews 2:3-4 AMP says:

> **Such a great salvation...was declared at first by the Lord [Himself], and it was confirmed to us and proved to be real and genuine by those who personally heard [Him speak].**
>
> **[Besides this evidence] it was also established and plainly endorsed by God, Who showed His approval of it by signs and wonders and various miraculous manifestations of [His] power and by imparting the gifts of the Holy Spirit [to the believers] according to His own will.**

51

The *Marvins*

The name "Marvin" was brought forth by the Holy Spirit off and on for a few days while we were in prayer.

We were preparing for a meeting in Wisconsin, and we wanted to stop at a certain roadside restaurant for breakfast.

As we were getting out of the beautiful Cadillac Vicki had bought for us, we noticed a couple waving to us from across the parking lot.

We did not recognize them, but as we approached the restaurant, they smiled at us and we stood in line together waiting for tables.

When the waitress signaled them to a table, they invited us to sit with them as the restaurant was quite crowded. We accepted.

"We waved to you because we saw your beautiful Cadillac—same model as ours, but in such great condition!" they stated.

They continued, "The road salt and ice-melting products have taken their toll on our car."

Noting that we had a Texas license plate, they inquired about our whereabouts, and they were curious about what we

did in Texas, how the winters were there and what we did for a living.

Phillip said, "We are about the business of the Lord Jesus Christ, and I am a minister of the gospel. We are on our way to a meeting fifty miles away."

The couple, who had been so enthusiastic, suddenly became very quiet.

The lady said she could never get her husband to their Lutheran church unless it was for a wedding or a funeral of some relative.

The man bowed his head and admitted he didn't get anything out of church.

When we explained the difference between being a good church member and knowing the forgiveness of sin that Jesus offers, tears came to his eyes.

It was easy to lead them to the knowledge of our Lord Jesus.

The wife realized all her faithful attendance and observance of infant sprinkling and confirmation could not assure her of eternal salvation.

Her husband found the joy of sins forgiven! We met them with enthusiasm over material things, but we left them with positive and eternal values secured!

We realized we hadn't even introduced ourselves. We told them our names and the area where we lived in Minnesota.

They said, "We are Mr. and Mrs. Lee Marvin!"

What a privilege and an honor to be a cog in God's machinery—winning the lost!

> So repent (change your mind and purpose); turn around and return [to God], that your sins may be erased (blotted out, wiped clean), that times of refreshing (of recovering from the effects of heat, of reviving with fresh air) may come from the presence of the Lord.
>
> **Acts 3:19** AMP

52

Ladies *Only*

We heard Billye Brim was going to be in Paynesville, Minnesota, at a camp, so we called and made motel reservations. We didn't know Billye very well at this time.

Sister Jeanne Wilkerson was to be there also. We had been in Sister Wilkerson's home many times for prayer.

The phone rang, and it was Billye.

She said, "Brother Halverson, Sister Jeanne Wilkerson was supposed to come and minister with me, but she is unable to attend. Would you and Fern pray about coming to Paynesville and ministering at this convention?"

"Billye!" Phillip exclaimed. "We just completed plans to attend and have made motel reservations. We'll certainly be there!"

Billye said, "This is a most unusual invitation, because it's strictly a women's meeting, and men aren't even allowed on the premises. We will alert all the guards at the gates.

"You will have a cottage all by yourselves, and your meals will be provided."

Phillip said, "Of course we'll be there. We'll do whatever has to be done."

We knew God was in the arranging of our being there, first, because if Billye says it, you know she heard God say it. Second, we had already made plans to be there.

There are no preparations you can make for a meeting that is organized by the Holy Ghost. You have to be utterly dependent upon Him that you are in the right place at the right time.

Phillip would never go to a platform without me. I thought, *He wants me nearby in case he can't think of anything to say!* You see, I talk, but he's quieter.

However, he was never quiet when it came to talking about the things of God. When he's through he just looks at me and smiles, and whatever I have on my heart I'm to share.

Billye began to introduce us for the morning meeting of the second day. She began to talk about the quickening of the Holy Spirit to bring about His plan.

Billye said, "There are many here who have felt that first faint quickening of a new life within you. Every woman here who is pregnant, even though you've not revealed it to anyone, come forward and Brother Halverson is going to pray for you."

What a surprise for both Phillip and me! Those women streamed to the front. Phillip was going to lay hands on them and bless each of them in her labor and in her delight of a new baby.

As he reached in their direction, before he could even touch them, they began to fall—frontwards, backwards, sideways.

It seemed like some of the women who were obviously pregnant sailed through the air a little bit before they landed.

Phillip said, "I never saw anything like it anyplace or even ever heard of it." He was frightened.

Since that time we've had many mothers come up to us at services in different places and display their babies to us with great joy.

Phillip never even prayed for them. I don't remember him saying one word about their deliveries being easy.

God wants to reveal things to us in the Spirit. You know how a husband whispers something to his wife—for instance, "I love you"?

God does that too. He whispers things to us in our inner man and tells us things that we need to know.

Blessed shall be the fruit of thy body....

Deuteronomy 28:4

53

Delivered from *Drugs*

Billye Brim had asked Phillip and me if we would consider coming to share at a meeting to be held in Los Angeles in 1983.

It doesn't take a lot to want to be with Billye. You almost don't have to pray about it because it's so delightful to be with her.

But we did lay it before the Lord, and it seemed good to us and to the Holy Ghost, so we gave our consent.

A few days before the three-day meeting was to take place, Brother Kenneth Copeland announced the meeting on his TV program. Suddenly, almost every hotel room around that area was filled.

"Three Days of Glory!" had become a historic event in the Spirit!

People not connected to us, driving by on the freeway, thought the Los Angeles Convention Center where we were was on fire and reported it to us.

On the second day, on one floor below us, a large Catholic youth group was having a meeting. But many of the youth

came up on the escalators to our meeting, where they received Jesus as Savior, and many were baptized in the Holy Ghost!

It is impossible for me to transmit the intensity of the fervor that flowed over us.

It was an awesome time. There were too many manifestations to recall all of them.

The afternoon of the last day, Brother Wilkerson sat next to Phillip on the front row as Billye was preaching. He was writing continually.

Phillip thought this was interesting because the previous night the Holy Spirit had been interceding about "writing, writing, writing."

We did not know at that time who this man was, but at the end of the meeting he introduced himself as Pastor Wilkerson of Melodyland, in Anaheim, California.

Well, of course, we had heard of him and his church.

"Brother Kenneth Copeland called me," Pastor Wilkerson said, "and said if I would ask you to minister in my church next Sunday you would accept."

"We are already scheduled to minister at a church next Sunday morning," Phillip replied.

"Would you come to Melodyland for the Sunday night service then?" Pastor Wilkerson asked.

(People later told us, "You don't pray about going to Melodyland! *Everyone* wants to be invited there!")

The following Sunday morning, just as Phillip and I got up to minister and had fastened our microphones, suddenly I felt terribly nauseated. I knew if I didn't exit quickly I would become ill on the platform.

Looking for a near exit as I unfastened my mike, I noticed a "hippie type" young man at the left rear of the church. He got up and headed for the front doors.

By this time I was dashing out with the pastor's wife right behind me. I made it to the ladies' room and quickly relieved myself of the nausea and rinsed my mouth.

Then I went to my husband, refastened my mike and continued.

I observed this same young man come back in to take his former seat. The Holy Spirit spoke to me, *Drugs.*

I spoke out that someone was there (or possibly several people were there) who needed deliverance from drugs. I said, "I know who you are, and if you don't come, I'll come and get you."

Instantly that young man left his seat and came to stand in front of Phillip. The power and demonstration of the Holy Ghost were in evidence as we ministered to him. He went down under the almighty power of God, and we did too. It took a while.

Others came for deliverance from alcohol and tobacco. This was a Holy Ghost meeting.

The pastor's wife told us on our way back to the hotel that this young man's family had spent over $100,000 on various drug treatments, to no avail.

Three or four weeks later, while attending Brother Yandian's church in Tulsa, this same California pastor's wife came to talk to us.

She was attending Brother Hagin's seminar the following week, since she was a Rhema graduate.

She exclaimed, talking about the drug addict who had been delivered in our service at her church, "You wouldn't know him! He has cut his long hair, shaved off his long beard, cut off his wrist chains, now wears a business suit and has a good job."

Therefore if any man be in Christ, he is a new creature: old things are passed away; behold, all things are become new.

2 Corinthians 5:17

54

Melodyland—
Dr. Wilkerson

Pastor Wilkerson sent a limousine to pick us up that Sunday afternoon to drive us through some beautiful scenery near Melodyland in Anaheim.

Melodyland is huge. It has a large center platform, with tiers of seats encircling it.

After the music, just before we were to go up the five or six steps to the platform, I turned to Phillip and said, "I believe I am to begin. Do you think so?"

"Yes," he replied, "you begin."

The first words that came out of my mouth were ones I never intended to say. I heard them for the first time: *"We are to transact business for God!"*

Then I paused, as I didn't know what to say next, but more came.

"This is going to be a different service. While we are giving you what the Holy Spirit is giving us, you are going to be moved upon to come to the foot of the platform steps and give money in the offering."

Amazed at what I was saying, I continued, "It will be a flow of the Spirit and not an interruption while we speak."

Looking to Dr. Wilkerson, I asked him if it would be okay to leave the offering buckets during the meeting at the intervals where they had been placed around the platform.

"Anything you say!" was his enthusiastic reply. (The regular offering had already been taken.)

Remember, we knew absolutely nothing about that church, except that it was big.

During the time we ministered, people came from all over the congregation, quietly descending steps to place an offering in the bucket. Then they quietly returned to their seats.

The anointing to minister was evident in our delivery.

At the close of this lengthy service, Dr. Wilkerson announced, "The Halversons will be with us again tomorrow night. Don't miss it!"

He hadn't checked with us. The Holy Ghost had different directions, and we left the next morning.

A month or so later we were in an evening service at Rhema and Dr. Wilkerson was seated a couple of rows ahead of us.

When the meeting was over, he came to talk with us.

"Have you heard the results of your meeting in Melodyland?" he inquired.

"We haven't heard a thing," Phillip replied.

Then he related to us that because of the many mortgages on the enormous Melodyland property between Disneyland and Knott's Berry Farm, they were in deep financial trouble and faced the possibility of losing the church.

On the Saturday following our meeting, they had to come up with $1,000,000 in order to buy time to raise the rest of the debt money.

Not knowing anything of this, the Holy Spirit set Phillip and me up to receive a supernatural offering.

Dr. Wilkerson said, "By Saturday we had surpassed the needed funds, and the church was saved! People came in all week with big checks.

"I didn't know you folks had a financial ministry," he said.

We replied, "We don't, but God does!"

God is able to make all grace abound toward you....

2 Corinthians 9:8

55

The Emergency *Room*

Many times in Minnesota in the dead of winter, our son Jim would be up at 5:30 in the morning to go to Minnehaha Academy, a Christian Covenant High School six blocks from our home.

His love for ice hockey often overcame his need for food and sleep.

When you have a son active in senior sports, you already know that the head coach doesn't call a mother to report an insignificant nosebleed, a black eye or anything short of fatal disaster.

That is why I was alarmed to hear the voice of Jim Baxter, head coach, tell me over the phone that Jim had experienced a blow to his head while playing hockey.

Since all efforts to revive him were futile, they were taking him immediately to the emergency room at the University of Minnesota Hospital, four miles away.

Phillip walked in the door as I hung up the phone, and together we prayed and rebuked the devil's attempts to harm our son in any way. Then we hightailed it to the emergency room.

We were only a couple of minutes behind the coach when we arrived at the hospital.

The nurses were cutting off Jim's heavy clothes and preparing him for surgery.

Our son was "out of it"—eyes wide open and body rigid.

Without hesitation, Phillip placed his hands on Jim's head and said, "In the name of Jesus, intervene, O God, in Jesus' mighty name."

Immediately, Jim, who had been lying motionless, raised his arm to his head as he began to raise himself up.

"My head hurts! My head hurts!" he cried in anguish.

The other medical help in the room were as astonished as we were to the immediate response of the flesh to the command in the Spirit. A hush fell.

Dr. French, a leading brain specialist, had just come into the hospital—one day earlier than he was scheduled—and "happened" to be right there.

He informed us that Jim had a severe skull depression and the dangers included brain fluid leaking from the brain sac. That's why surgery was imperative, and he would perform it.

"We can't tell from the X rays whether fluid is leaking or not, so we want to go in and remedy the situation, which can be potentially fatal," said Dr. French.

"How long will it take?" Phillip inquired.

"Anywhere from twenty minutes to three hours, depending on what we find," was the doctor's response.

"You saw Jim respond just now. We will only give you permission to make an incision to determine if fluid is leaking," Phillip said.

"Fine," replied the doctor, "let's hope for the best."

In twenty minutes or less, out came Jim with a bandage on his head.

The doctor announced, "Jim is very fortunate to have suffered that deep a depression without the bone splintering and puncturing the dura mater, causing spinal fluid leakage."

We had been confronted with a serious lifetime disability, but we did what we read to do in God's Word:

> **My Father will grant you whatever you ask in My name.... Ask and keep on asking and you will receive, so that your joy (gladness, delight) may be full and complete.**
>
> **John 16:23,24 AMP**

There were no complications. I sat up in a chair in Jim's hospital room that night, and when Dr. French came in that next morning, Jim asked, "Can I play hockey?"

"Sure! We'll take that bandage off in three or four days, and you can join your hockey team."

That very evening we accompanied Jim to a hockey game!

Jim's love for hockey is still constant. Now he coaches hockey for the Minnesota Squirts, and many of the young boys become members of his church because of his love for them, the game, but most of all, for Jesus!

56

Changed *Directions*

As we began to travel more, when we would arrive back at our home, we were welcomed by our great friends, Gordy and Donna Nylin.

They weren't ordinary friends. They were very special friends! They devoted themselves to us.

I had been an altar worker for many years in an A.A. Allen tent meeting in Minneapolis, and Donna was one of the ladies I gave Scriptures to and prayed with.

I always followed up with a note to remind the person of the Lord's commitment to them and encouraged them to find a church of their choice. This is how I met Donna.

Gordy was a very good, upright Lutheran man. He taught Sunday school, but he was hesitant to embrace the "full gospel."

He had called Phillip one Friday and asked if he could come over on Saturday.

"Sure, Gordy, you come on over," Phillip said, knowing all good Norwegians like to have coffee and talk.

I was busy inside the house, and when Phil came back inside later he said, "Oh, Gordy just gave his heart to the Lord and shed tears of repentance when we prayed!"

We rejoiced together and didn't see or hear from them until we noticed Gordy and Donna at church. They invited us to Sunday dinner with their children and our son, Jim.

A couple of weeks later, Gordy called and asked if he and Donna could come one evening. "Sure! Come on," we replied.

"We want our children to be under the influence of you and Fern," Gordy said.

"To provide for anything that could happen, we would like to have you be in position to see to it that our children are raised properly and our money is spent for their education, being in your trust."

We were completely surprised. What an honor! To be entrusted with their two precious children, in case of an emergency, was very humbling indeed.

That is a preface to what I want to relate further.

I had always encouraged Phillip, an outdoorsman with an indoor job, to hunt and fish (I love to fish too), and as a result, we built three different cabins on three different lakes in Minnesota and Wisconsin.

Gordy and his son, Joe, were always on hand to help put in footings and foundations.

Donna and I prepared and served the food.

Three cabins later, we had formed a friendship that is rare.

Gordy was a faithful friend, not only in helping and setting aside his own time, but he and Donna excelled in entertaining us. Gordy's specialty was treating us at very nice restaurants.

He made it difficult for us to reciprocate, although we tried.

Phillip and I wanted to take a couple of weeks of vacation, and since neither of us had ever been in Florida, we made plans and looked up routes to go on a certain day. Gordy and Donna went with us.

Headed south, we arrived in Memphis to spend the night in a motel.

Over breakfast the next morning, Phillip shared with Gordy and Donna that he had prayed much during the night for "M.J." Over and over, the Holy Spirit named this person, whom we scarcely knew, being a friend of a friend.

"Well, Phillip," Gordy said authoritatively, "if you want to leave here and head for M.J. in Tulsa, we'll just forget about Florida and do as you feel God wants you to do."

"Oh, Gordy!" exclaimed Phillip, "I would never ask you to change your vacation plans, which we are involved with too."

"Let's go and find M.J. in Tulsa," Gordy announced to all of us.

After breakfast we headed west instead of south, traveling that day through the beautiful state of Arkansas.

When we arrived in Tulsa, we checked into a motel.

We couldn't remember M.J.'s last name—but finally it came to me, so we phoned them.

"You mean you are here in Tulsa?" the voice on the other end of the phone asked.

"We want to see you before you leave. How long will you be here?" M.J.'s wife inquired.

"We want to see you and M.J. too. Why don't you come to the motel, and we can visit?"

"M.J. says he isn't going anywhere!" was her reply.

"Well, just tell M.J. that I changed my travel plans, and instead of going to Florida, I came over here just to see him," Phillip instructed her.

They arrived—not as we'd known them previously—but changed! She was nervous and apprehensive about her husband but tried to be welcoming and cordial.

M.J., on the other hand, wouldn't look up. He was utterly dejected, not dressed neatly and sharply as usual. He kept his head down, looking only at the floor.

We sat on the opposite bed, and Phillip extended his hand and clasped M.J.'s hand.

He told him of the urgency of the Holy Spirit and emphasized how Gordy had reinforced the decision to come to Tulsa.

At that point, M.J. began to cry loudly, agonizingly, bawling like a baby and telling us about this strangeness that had come over him.

"My wife doesn't know anything about this. I have tried unsuccessfully to commit suicide.

"I have waited at the street curb for a lot of traffic and then darted out in front of large trucks. Each time the trucks have managed to swerve and avoid hitting me.

"I figured it would be a quick way to go, and it would get me out of a home environment," M.J. related.

By that time, we were all in tears. His wife kept saying, "Oh, M.J., I can't believe you did such a thing! This is unbelievable. Oh, no!"

Phillip assured M.J. that God had sent him to deliver him from this demonic attack.

Not only did M.J. repent of his negligence of God's Word and prayer, but he repented of giving the devil's thoughts such a wide entrance.

They left us singing with joy unspeakable and full of glory! Both M.J. and his wife were restored.

We took in Brother Hagin's meetings and spent some time in the beautiful hills and mountains of Arkansas and Branson, Missouri, and had a wonderful time together.

A friend loveth at all times....

Proverbs 17:17

57

"Sold" by an *Angel*

At one time we had purchased a lakeshore lot from a widower who lived out of state.

During the winter months, we and some of Jim's friends cleared land for a cabin site, enjoying the huge wood fires amidst the deep snow. The slope to the lake was very steep.

Although this was a much sought-after lake with good fishing, sailboating and swimming, we felt by the time spring arrived, we would not enjoy such a steep bank.

We also felt we could use the money for more worthwhile things than building a cabin.

There was only one other cabin nearby—a new one that an older couple had built to be their retirement dream.

The Bensons were very nice neighbors.

I wanted them to be the first to know of our decision to sell, and the day that we called on them, Mrs. Benson informed us that her husband was substituting for a friend at the local gas station.

As we filled our car with gas, we had the opportunity to tell Mr. Benson of our decision to sell our lot. He appeared to be disinterested, but we felt it was the courteous thing to do.

That evening at home we talked about placing an ad in the local paper.

The very next morning as we were finishing our breakfast, an old beat-up truck clattered into our driveway in a heavy rain. It was the Bensons.

Welcoming our offer of fresh coffee, they were anxious to tell us they wanted to buy our lot and wanted to know what we wanted for it.

We couldn't have been more surprised! Before we could tell them what we hoped to get, they made us an offer for far more than we dreamed we could sell it for.

They were so anxious that we took our deed and pertinent papers to their attorney's office the next day to complete the sale.

Mr. Benson brought cash in a box. They were delighted to obtain this lot.

It was only outside the lawyer's office as we were ready to part that I asked Mr. Benson what use he had for the lot or what plans he had in mind.

"Well," he replied, "yesterday morning I noticed a man walking on your lot very early in the morning. I went over to meet him, and he proceeded to tell me what a special lot it was—such a great beach, full of hardwoods, privacy at that end of the lake and a good investment.

"I determined to get it since you told me you wanted to sell."

We never did find out who that "man" was. We believe it was an angel!

> **Behold, I send an Angel before you to keep and guard you on the way and to bring you to the place I have prepared.**
>
> **Exodus 23:20 AMP**

58

Surgery *Prevented*

Reverend Randy and Roberta Morrison, pastors of a rapidly growing church in Minneapolis, were sharing a time of prayer with us.

Phillip, looking at Randy, began speaking by the Spirit. Several times he said, "I loose that surgery! Surgery, be loosed in Jesus' name."

Then, looking at Roberta, Phillip said, "You are going to have another son."

Randy's sudden response was "That is impossible! I've had a vasectomy."

They protested, telling us about how content they were with just one son, Topaz.

However, after ministering in their church one evening, we met in the privacy of their office, where Roberta announced that she was indeed pregnant.

Randy's doctor was baffled.

During Roberta's pregnancy, Phillip sensed the powers of darkness attempting to interfere with the child's development. He frequently prayed for the baby.

In the hospital, after the birth, Randy brought his new son, Tyrone, to us.

Phillip held him, cuddled him and lifted him up both with his hands and with urgent prayer. Among other things, he said that Tyrone would have a prophetic anointing.

Later, Roberta told us, "I saw a rainbow over Tyrone's crib in the hospital, and the Holy Spirit told me, *He will have no more surgeries.*

"I didn't know what this meant," she said.

But then at six months, the doctor reported that Tyrone had Hirschsprung's disease, which would require surgery.

After that surgery, the doctor said to expect several more surgeries.

Roberta said, "Oh, no! He'll never have another one! God has spoken to me."

The doctor looked at her sincerely and said, "Most of the children who have this disease don't grow very tall and are very skinny."

Nevertheless, at a very early age, Tyrone entered vigorously into praise and worship with his family.

Then he began to preach. At first, he preached to imaginary audiences in their home. His dedication and his grasp of Scripture fascinated Randy and Roberta.

Just as the Holy Spirit had spoken through Phillip, they saw a prophetic anointing on Tyrone at an early age.

Today, Tyrone is a fine young man, a joy to everyone and is obviously destined to continue to be mightily used of God.

At sixteen, he was six feet nine inches tall, and he is still growing!

He loves basketball and has trained with a former NBA player who attends their church.

Tyrone recently asked this man, "Do you read your Bible every day?"

The athlete replied, "No."

"That's more important than basketball!" Tyrone informed him.

I'm so glad we serve a God who isn't limited by man's words! The doctor had pronounced disease, multiple surgeries and stunted growth over Tyrone.

But God had a purpose for Tyrone. He had called him, and just as Romans 11:29 AMP says:

> **God's gifts and His call are irrevocable. [He never withdraws them when once they are given, and He does not change His mind about those to whom He gives His grace or to whom He sends His call.]**

59

Courthouse *Prayer*

I was invited to perform a wedding in Tulsa in the fall and had to go to the Minneapolis courthouse to get a copy of my ordination papers to send to the officials in Tulsa.

The clerk that waited on me accepted my three dollars and left the counter to go to another room.

Through the wide window I saw another clerk working at a desk, and nearby stood a well-dressed man whom I imagined to be a supervisor.

He was obviously displeased about something because he let loose a stream of words that would make anyone blush.

I could hear him using the names of God and Jesus in vain, as well as mentioning hell and damning people.

The clerk who had taken my request came back to tell me the copy machine had broken down and she would have to go into another department.

"Do you have the time to wait?" she asked.

I assured her I did, sensing the Lord wanted me specifically there.

The other clerk conferred with her and also accompanied her to the other department.

Only the gentleman was left, and he came right over to the window I was waiting at and opened a record book.

No one else was around.

"I understand that you are a religious man," I said.

"What would ever give you that idea?" he responded.

"Well, I heard you using words that are found only in the Bible, so I figured you were quite religious," I replied.

"I did?" he said incredulously.

"Yes," I replied, "words like Jesus Christ, God, hell and I even heard you damning something to hell—actually consigning it to hell!"

"I did?" was his wondering response.

The copy machine didn't get fixed, and the clerks were detained elsewhere until I had the opportunity to tell him about his chances of making hell and his opportunity to make heaven *now!*

I had the distinct privilege of hearing the gentleman pray the sinner's prayer and thanking me for talking to him.

The righteous are bold as a lion.

Proverbs 28:1

60

My Oriental *Brother*

The first experience I had standing in line at the bank on a Saturday morning was in a chilling January wind with five people ahead of me.

I could hear the teller talking through her speaker to the person on the other side of the window, the first one in my line.

From my view, he appeared short with straight, shiny black hair, and when I heard his speech, I knew he was Oriental.

"I'm sorry," said the crisp, efficiently trained voice of the teller, as she passed his check back to him. "We cannot cash your check because you do not have an account with this bank."

Have you ever put yourself in the other fellow's boots? I did. It seemed almost as if *I* had received that disappointing news. I could picture a family without funds for the weekend.

I stepped out of line just as he did and walked over a few steps to him. "Tell me, Sir," I said, "how much is your check for?"

I noted it was a University of Minnesota check (If that isn't good, we are all in big trouble!), and that it was for twenty-five dollars.

"I'll cash your check for you," I said, and asked him to endorse it.

He turned it over and showed me he already had.

So I took twenty-five dollars out of my cash deposit and handed it to him. He was surprised and quiet.

"Tell me," I said, "have you ever heard of Jesus Christ?"

A big smile came across his face as he pointed to himself and said, "Me, Christian!"

Bear ye one another's burdens, and so fulfil the law of Christ.

Galatians 6:2

Within ten minutes I had deposited his check with others in my ministry account, and it didn't cost me a penny!

61

A Job *Breakthrough*

En route back to our home in Tulsa, I was changing planes at the Atlanta airport. I settled myself into an aisle seat.

Refreshing times with five other sisters in the Lord were now memories as I eagerly looked forward to joining my husband, Phillip, from whom I had never been separated before.

A fine-looking young black man sat next to me in the window seat.

As the plane took off, I introduced myself to him.

He said, "My name is Terry."

"Where are you headed, Terry?" I asked.

"I was planning to go to Dallas to look for work, but I have decided on Tulsa, where I hear job opportunities are better," he replied.

How could I help him? I knew a good contact.

I told Terry, "My Father is very influential. Would you like me to mention your need of a job to Him?"

"Oh," he replied, "would you?"

Would I!

I took his hand in mine, closed my eyes and said, "Father, in Jesus' name, I ask You to give Terry the best job he could ever hope for. Thank You, Father. Amen."

A surprised and delighted Terry shook my hand and said, "All right, Mama!"

It turned out he was a Christian, and I had the privilege of agreeing with my brother!

We did the very best thing we could do—we let our requests be made known to God and the two of us agreed as touching one thing! The result was certain!

If two of you shall agree on earth as touching any thing that they shall ask, it shall be done for them of my Father which is in heaven.

Matthew 18:19

62

Washington, D. C.'s
'Think Tanks'

I stand in many different kinds of lines regularly: banking lines, voting lines, airport lines, grocery lines and so forth.

On this particular day I found myself at the end of a long bank line that wound back and forth several times.

A well-dressed older woman ahead of me had two attaché cases, one on each side, which she moved up a few inches each time the line moved.

When she turned toward me and smiled, I asked her, "Are your bags heavy? Can I help you?"

She thanked me, said they were not heavy, but she was on her way to the airport and just stopped to get some cash. She had formerly lived in my area.

Being of a curious nature, I asked her where she was flying.

"Washington, D.C." was her reply.

"Oh," I said, "I don't know anyone who lives in D.C. Are you going to visit?"

"No," she replied, "I am going to Washington on business."

"Business! What kind of business are you in?" I asked.

She told me she operated *"think tanks."*

I had a vague idea about think tanks, having heard of advertising people getting together for sessions where everyone says any idea that comes to mind about a certain product. At the end of an hour or so, they assess what would be the most productive ad. That is all I knew.

Sensing that the Holy Spirit wanted to reach this woman, I continued, aware that the lines on each side of us were now in on our interesting conversation.

"Please tell me about think tanks in our nation's capital," I urged.

She proceeded to tell me about all the prominent people from the state of Minnesota who came to her sessions.

She drew herself up as tall as she could while she announced the honors that had been conferred upon her.

We definitely had an audience.

As we slowly moved forward inches at a time, there was a quiet moment when I was looking to the Lord for His specific direction.

This woman needed help, although to look at her impressive attire and to hear the authority in her voice you wouldn't guess it.

Suddenly, when she turned toward me, I touched her arm and said, "I am very interested in your opinion. You give them out to others. Would you give me your opinion on a certain matter?"

"Of course, I will be happy to do that. What did you have in mind?" she asked.

"Tell me," I said, "what is your opinion of Jesus Christ?"

Her face fell dramatically and she got a puzzled look on her face. She became somewhat agitated and said, "I think He was a good man."

"Well, Jesus Himself said that there was only One Who was good and that was His Father. He wouldn't let people call Him good," was my reply.

She said, "Just the same, I say He was a good man."

"But Jesus was more than a good man," I continued. "He claimed to be the Son of God—the only Son of God. Do you believe that?"

I can tell you, we definitely had an audience!

Her agitation increased as the Holy Spirit was moving in to the *truth*. "He did a lot of good," was her only reply.

"I want to know," I pressed, "was He who He said He was—the Son of God—or was He a liar? Who was Jesus?" I asked.

She didn't answer. She didn't want to call Jesus a liar.

But immediately, the tall man just ahead of her turned completely around to me, nodding his head, wide-eyed, and said, "I believe Jesus was who He said He was."

The Holy Spirit had reached him!

The woman was confronted by the *truth.* I pray the faithful Holy Spirit will continue as the "Hound of Heaven" to pursue her.

The man was also confronted by a decision, and he immediately made the right response.

How many others in that line had to make a decision?

Remember, *unbelief is refusing to believe what you hear.*

For God so loved the world, that he gave his only begotten Son, that whosoever believeth in him should not perish, but have everlasting life.

For God sent not his Son into the world to condemn the world; but that the world through him might be saved.

John 3:16,17

63

Making

To facilitate boarding for a flight the next day, I went to the Minneapolis airport to pick up a prepaid ticket furnished by a church out East.

As I took my turn in a line of about eight people, I could overhear a young soldier talking with great earnestness to a desk attendant.

He had a government check in his hand, and he had twenty-five minutes to get on a plane. His destination was Fort Hood, Texas.

I heard the clerk explain that they did not cash checks at the airport and that he should have thought of that earlier.

I remembered how Phillip had had to "make camp" in time when he'd been in the service.

Bolstered by my experience in the bank line, cashing the $25 check for the Oriental man, I stepped out of line alongside this nervous young soldier.

"How much is your check for, young man?" I asked.

When he showed me a $235 check, I hesitated.

Then suddenly I had an idea! I asked the clerk if she would accept my credit card if I bought his ticket.

"Of course!"

I asked the young man if he would accept my check for the difference.

In other words, his fare was $188, which I would put on my credit card. He would endorse his government check to me, and I would write him my personal check for the $47 difference.

A very happy soldier said, "Of course!"

The clerk got the ticket out of the computer in a few minutes, and just before the soldier took off, he said, "God bless you, Lady!"

What he didn't realize was that I now had his name, serial number and address.

I knew he would never forget that moment in his life, and as he turned to run for his plane, I asked him if he had ever heard of Jesus Christ.

"Yes, Ma'am!" was his reply.

I wrote to this young soldier, lovingly explaining the way of salvation and thanking the Father for an opportunity to show His love and concern.

Fear thou not; for I am with thee: be not dismayed; for I am thy God: I will strengthen thee; yea, I will help thee; yea, I will uphold thee with the right hand of my righteousness.

Isaiah 41:10

64

The Voting *Place*

In November 1985, having moved back to Minnesota, I found myself at the neighborhood school, our polling place.

Several neighbors whom I hadn't seen for a few years greeted me. I told them of Phillip's transition to heaven.

As I took my place at the end of the line, a very well-dressed gentleman ahead of me asked, "Do you live around here?"

Looking out the window, I could see my house across the park, but I said, "Doesn't everyone?" as I didn't want to tell a perfect stranger where I lived.

He volunteered all kinds of information about himself. He owned a lot of property in other states, vast apartment projects and businesses.

"The taxes are higher in Minnesota, so I am thinking of selling my home. Maybe you've seen it on the corner—the new home on River Drive," he said.

"That is a beauty," I responded. "We watched it being built a few years ago."

Then I continued, "But why do you want to move else-where, just to save some taxes, because while our Minnesota taxes are higher than some states, we do give a lot of our money in services. Plus, we take care of the poor and needy people in a very fine way."

"I want to conserve my holdings and save every penny I possibly can in order to build up my estate!"

When he said "estate," the Holy Spirit alerted me.

"I was just reading," I said, "about a man like you. He had a lot of property and barns, and he sat down to figure out how he could increase his wealth and build even bigger barns.

"What that man didn't know was that very day his soul would be required of him. He had to leave it all."

I continued, emphasizing the uncertainty of life and pointing out that he had no assurance he would be able to open the door to his house just a block away.

> **But rather seek ye the kingdom of God; and all these things shall be added unto you. Fear not, little flock; for it is your Father's good pleasure to give you the kingdom.**
>
> **Sell that ye have, and give alms; provide yourselves bags which wax not old, a treasure in the heavens that faileth not, where no thief approacheth, neither moth corrupteth. For where your treasure is, there will your heart be also.**
>
> **Luke 12:31-34**

65

A Curse *Broken*

My Aunt Edith and Uncle Frank invited me over for dinner one evening. I loved being with them occasionally and looked forward to the comfort of their home.

Phillip had gone to be with the Lord only a month earlier.

After a nice meal, they said a lady they had met at their church was coming over after her work in a hospital.

After this lady arrived, our conversation soon revolved around her husband, who, she said "was perpetually drunk, unemployed and abusive to her."

She thought it was beyond her strength to keep the relationship going. (They had moved to Minneapolis the previous year.)

The Holy Spirit was speaking to me while this lady was talking.

I was aware of a spirit of the occult in the family and inquired further into her background.

"Did you ever go to a fortune-teller?" I inquired.

"Yes, back in Massachusetts a friend and I went into a fortune-teller's house just for the fun of it," she replied.

Her story of their home back East was one of possible envy to most people.

Her husband had an excellent job. She was a socialite and a volunteer for many organizations.

"Suddenly everything changed," she continued.

"My faithful husband became morose and unpredictable. Our move here, to be with our only daughter, has been a nightmare."

Wiping the tears from her weary face, she told of a husband who lounged around, wouldn't work and made life miserable for her and her daughter.

She'd had to find employment—only to come home to an intolerable situation. The last three months had been horrible.

"I don't know what to do," she stated pathetically.

"Tell me what that fortune-teller said to you," I inquired, sensing the urging of the Holy Spirit.

"That first visit was interesting," she declared. "She told both of us about our past.

"She told me my husband was going to have a big job opportunity and asked if I could come back the next day.

"'When you come,' the fortune-teller told me, 'bring one of your husband's undergarments—or even a handkerchief— and a fresh, large, ripe tomato.'

"I was excited about this!" the woman said. "When my friend and I returned the next day, she unfolded the T-shirt I brought and in the middle of it she put the ripe tomato.

"In a flash," she continued, "the fortune-teller produced a sharp knife and severely and quickly pierced the tomato right on the white T-shirt.

"I was startled to say the least." Tears were now flowing.

I had the solution from the Holy Spirit.

Carefully, I explained how she had unwittingly turned her husband over to the evil forces of the devil, who graphically destroyed his ongoing life.

"When the fortune-teller slashed the tomato on his white T-shirt, she put an end to his family situation," I explained.

"Whatever can be done? What will I do?" this woman cried helplessly, as we were all moved with compassion for her, now a new believer.

Since I was in my aunt and uncle's home, I asked my uncle, "Can we step into the kitchen for a moment?

"We have to cast out the devilish spirits that affect this family's very future and plead the blood of Jesus over us all first. This can be broken.

"Uncle Frank, you have this authority in your own home, to set her and her family free right now!" I declared authoritatively.

But my uncle was hesitant. "Oh! I could never do that," he replied.

"The devil is a powerful being, and I don't feel I can have such a confrontation," was his protest.

He continued, "I have never seen such a thing done.

"Fern, you go ahead. I know you have had experience with casting out the devil. Please," he said urgently, "you do it!"

I had his permission, and as we sat down again with our friend, I read the Scriptures and explained how important it was that we "plead the blood of Jesus" (an old-fashioned phrase we used to use all the time).

"I am going to place my hands on your head as I expel these spirits," I explained to her. "Do I have your permission?"

Unhesitatingly she cried out, *"Oh, yes, please do whatever you have to do!"*

We covered ourselves with the blood of Jesus. The devil and his imps were expelled with great and loud authority, and this new believer almost fell into a heap in her chair.

We sang some songs in the Spirit and also in the natural— all about the power in Jesus' blood.

Right away she straightened up and seemed so composed and relaxed for the first time that evening. After some coffee and dessert, she left and I stayed overnight.

Early the next morning, our friend called.

"Do you know what I found when I opened the front door last night, after leaving your home?" she queried.

"My husband was his old self. He embraced me and, as though nothing unpleasant had ever happened, resumed a friendly conversation and was up early this morning to shower and have breakfast, declaring he was going to look for work."

Her voice trembled almost in unbelief at what was happening.

Our rejoicing knew no bounds! We got on our knees to thank our Father for His mighty provision for our welfare here on earth.

I was able to meet this woman, her lovely daughter and her handsome, joyful husband.

My aunt and uncle led him to the Lord, and he was beginning a new life.

I never go looking for the devil. I am too full of the presence of God and His Word.

But if I am confronted with a situation where God has to step in and release captives, I don't hesitate a second!

Christ hath redeemed us from the curse of the law, being made a curse for us.... That the blessing of Abraham might come on the Gentiles through Jesus Christ....

Galatians 3:13,14

66

President Kennedy's

Assassination

Phillip's family had come from a small town in another state, and his two brothers still lived in Dallas.

Since he sometimes hunted with them, he called them about the hunting season that was approaching.

"I want you to know that you are not to go hunting this season, especially with Oswald." (There was a man who hunted with them named Oswald Harper.)

"We always hunt with Oswald, Phil," they replied, "because he is such a good shot."

Phillip and I drove to their residences to warn them in person. It was a certainty.

"Well, this year, this season, do not hunt with Oswald. It's probably better if you don't hunt at all. Someone is going to get shot," Phillip continued. "Better not to go at all."

Phillip's brothers knew he wouldn't give them such a warning if it were not important. So they didn't make hunting plans with Oswald.

There were other words that came by the Holy Spirit as Phillip prayed: *President, Oswald, Elm Street, Dallas, rifle, killing....* All disconnected and with other things uttered by the Spirit.

The day President Kennedy's assassination took place, we were glued to our television sets. I remember seeing the enactment over and over again, and hearing repeatedly the very names and places Phillip had prayed about so much.

Phillip's brothers called him. One of his brothers, now deceased, was the *president* of a small egg company. That small firm was on *Elm Street* in *Dallas.*

Wonderment filled us. Prayer in the Spirit brought forth words of wisdom. Phillip's forthcoming ministry was being established.

Wherefore let him that speaketh in an unknown tongue pray that he may interpret.

1 Corinthians 14:13

67

A Bizarre *Visitation*

Phillip and I were startled as Billye Brim related some information to us.

"Pastor Art Aragon of California told me of a most bizarre experience that just occurred," Billye related.

She went on, "Phillip, were you aware that you walked right through one of his walls on a Sunday morning?"

"What?" Phillip exclaimed. "I did what? I know nothing about this man, nor have I ever heard his name before."

"I told him he should write it out and I gave him your address," Billye recounted.

A few days later, we received a lengthy letter from this pastor, and here is part of it:

> *On April 16* [1983], *I went to a ministers' meeting in which Billye Brim was the guest speaker. Before the meeting, Pastor Glen Curry of Now Faith Fellowship intro-duced me to Sister Billye. I began to share with her some things that were happening in our church. Upon conversing with her, the Lord compelled me to share with her some-thing that had happened to me on Sunday morning, April 10...somewhere between 7 and 7:30 A.M.*

I was neither awake nor asleep, but was lying in my bed in the Spirit. I became aware that I was under the power of God's presence. It was very quiet in my room; then through the wall you, Phil, walked into my room. You looked at me and came over and knelt on the bed and stretched your hands out toward me.... I heard you praying for me. You were making heavy intercession for me. There were a few times you would say, "The power of God, the power of God, the Spirit of His might."

At one point my wife, JoAnn, who was already up and had showered, came into the room to wake me up. As she entered the bedroom, you stopped praying and turned towards her and watched her as she came to my side and tried to wake me up for church that morning. She told me to get up, then walked out of the room. You were watching her the whole time.

As she left the room, you turned and started praying again, hands stretched out and making heavy intercession.... My wife entered the room again. At this time you got up from the bed and walked through the same wall you had come through. Once you left the room, I was able to get up.

Brother Phil, that Sunday morning I ministered under the strongest anointing I have ever ministered under. That morning there was a young man about twenty-two years of age who had come for the very first time. He stood up and came forth weeping, pleading for help. He had been going to a home where people were gathering, saying it was a Bible study, but it wasn't. They practiced drugs and sex.... This young man said he was told he was the Antichrist and there was no hope for him.... He was gloriously delivered. He gave his life to the Lord and fell under God's marvelous power. He lay there for ten or fifteen minutes, and when he got up God had given him his prayer language in the Spirit.

There have been many other things that have occurred since that morning....

Brother Phil, you will never know what a blessing you are to me. Thank you for your obedience to God. You are truly a pillar of strength.

In His love,
Art Aragon

Phillip and I marveled anew at the methods God uses to accomplish His purposes.

Phillip said, "Let's send him our itinerary for the two weeks we will be in California next month and see if we can meet. I am anxious to meet him face-to-face and hear more particulars."

We met at this pastor's church and had lunch with him and his wife. They related this same incident.

"We are still in awe over what happened," said the pastor, "and many other things that have occurred since then. Let me tell you the latest.

"We are experiencing such a strong move of the Holy Spirit, both in the church body of believers and also in our personal lives.

"Because the power of God was so evident in our church body, my assistant pastor and I decided we and our wives would get a hotel room for the day just to pray and lie before the Lord in utter devotion. We had no requests. We wanted to just present ourselves to our God.

"I have been in missionary work in a province in China for several years," he continued, "and carry those dear people on my heart, even though I have been in California for over ten years.

"While we spread around the room, we laid all other cares and matters aside and worshipped and praised Almighty God for His moving in our midst.

"I was earnestly praying in tongues with the others. I heard myself uttering Chinese dialect, with which I was familiar, and immediately I was carried away in the Spirit to the very area I had worked in years before.

"My assistant pastor accompanied me as I moved about from place to place.

"There was this familiar street where we entered to find this woman I knew, older but easily recognizable to me, and I to her!

"We carried on an intense conversation and went on across the dirt street to other people with whom I conveyed some messages. It was as though time had not elapsed since my previous departure.

"Suddenly I was back in the hotel room. It was 5:15 P.M. We had gone to prayer about 9:15 A.M. I was in a state of unspeakable quietness. I remained silent and in awe.

"As we gradually got up and seated ourselves, my assistant, with great fervor and amazement, began to relate:

"'While I was praying,' he said, 'I was carried away to a foreign land in the Orient. There were peasants around in the dirt streets and I was at your side.

"'Pastor, you talked with everyone in this foreign language with great earnestness, calling them by their names. You and I traveled around this area and met other people.

"'I don't know what to make of this,' he continued, 'but *I know I was there, then suddenly I am here!*'"

The effectual fervent prayer of a righteous man availeth much.

James 5:16

68

A Bizarre *Recovery*

The mail delivery revealed a thick letter from Pastor Terry, whom we had never heard of, and it was with amazement that we read what he had to tell us.

His writing was so close together we had to reread the letter several times to get the full impact.

Because his first name was Terry and he told about a cervical situation, I thought it was about a woman.

Later, we met at Billye Brim's Minneapolis "Secrets of Intercession" Convention, where we were speakers with her.

Brother Jim Kaseman was there, and we asked him if we could meet with this pastor so he could record the testimony. Brother Kaseman was enthusiastic about it, and here is what we learned.

Brother Terry had been in and out of hospitals for some time. He was in ill health.

This particular day while in the hospital, he was in intense pain. Nurses were attending him and preparations were made to operate on his neck, in hopes of curing the pain.

"I was screaming out in pain, although medication had been administered," he said.

"Suddenly I was being assaulted by demons, flying like bats from hell above my bed. They were diving toward me and threatening to attack me.

"In agony I found myself lifted above the bed, looking down at my body. There were two nurses, one of whom loudly called for the 'crash cart.'

"Immediately I felt tubes being pushed into my body, and many life-saving techniques were started."

"'Oh, we've lost him!' cried one nurse. 'No, there he is,' declared another. It went back and forth. In the meantime I was observing all this, looking down from the room's ceiling.

"Although I had never met Phillip Halverson, I had heard him speak and pray.

"God spoke to me while I was out of my body, floating, *Pray like Phil Halverson!*

"I did so from my unusual spiritual position!

"Immediately I was back in my body and Phillip and Fern appeared at my side. Phillip stretched his hands out over my body, and as he did, a fountain of glorious light sprang from my belly!

"The feeling I had was such extreme peace! The room suddenly became quiet. Even the nurses ceased their labors for me.

"Tubes were withdrawn from me," he continued, "as all my vital signs were perfectly normal.

"I spent a month or two," he told us at the hotel, "recuperating my full strength and resting."

The day Brother Jim Kaseman and Phillip and I met this pastor and his wife at the hotel, he was the picture of robust health.

We certainly had not been aware of any of this. But we rejoiced at God's bizarre ways of accomplishing His secret purposes.

> **Look carefully then how you walk! Live purposefully and worthily and accurately, not as the unwise and witless, but as wise (sensible, intelligent people).**
>
> **Ephesians 5:15 AMP**

69

In the Oval *Office*

The Holy Spirit moved mightily in Phillip's prayers—naming world leaders, presidents, governors and governments.

The names of ordinary people, most of whom we had never heard of, also came forth in prayer.

I recall one morning Phillip came into the kitchen, still in his pajamas. His eyes filled with tears. I waited to hear what he would say.

"Fern, I have had a vision or a dream about President Nixon."

I waited to hear what was going to come.

"I was transported to the Oval Office, where our president, Richard Nixon, was sitting with his head in his hands, leaning over his desk."

He continued, "I stood behind him and placed my hands on his shoulders, praying for him and praying in the Holy Spirit." Then Phillip was quiet for a while.

"We are going to hear our president resign today," said Phillip. "You will hear it shortly on the television news."

I turned on the local news station to find a report of "breaking news." There was President Nixon, with his face drawn from the struggle he had been through, announcing his resignation.

The experience shook both of us. We told no one about this until years later, and then only in private to friends.

> **For with stammering lips and another tongue will he speak to this people.**
>
> **Isaiah 28:11**

70

Santa *Rosa*

Billye Brim and I were holding meetings in Santa Rosa, California, at Pastor Watson Argue's church.

Billye was impressed to leave on the night flight the evening of our last meeting to be with her desperately ill husband.

I was to finish that last night, and I knew it before she asked me.

We had lunch with Pastor and Mrs. Argue that day.

Just before Brother and Sister Argue were to pick me up that evening at the motel, I became very dizzy and nauseous.

Billye had already departed for her home in Collinsville, Oklahoma.

When the Argues knocked, I barely made it to the door and told them of this sudden experience.

"Pray for me," I said. "Satan just wants to oppose this meeting tonight."

Brother Argue did pray for me, rebuking Satan and the cause of my condition.

We stopped on the way to church and I became ill on the side of the road.

I was so dizzy when we arrived at the church that the ushers had to steady me as I got to the pastor's office.

I asked the pastor to send an usher for me before I was to speak, to hold me up until I grasped the podium and then I would be okay. I had to assure them this was the way it was to be.

The usher came for me. In the natural, I would never imagine myself standing up and addressing an audience in my condition.

But when my hands grasped the pulpit, I felt strong— not at all dizzy.

We had a great meeting. The gifts of the Spirit flowed through me with the word of wisdom and the word of knowledge.

Just as I was finished and announced that I had delivered all the Lord had given me for that meeting, terrible nausea gripped me again.

With a glance at the pastor in the front row, I headed for an open door to an outer court just outside the platform, where I became ill again, then returned to the platform.

The anointing of the Holy Spirit was evident.

When Pastor Argue saw me walk back to the platform, not dizzy, he urged the people to come forward and I would lay hands on them.

I had no intention of doing this. However, at the pastor's direction, I asked for a chair to sit down at the edge of the one-step platform.

As the people passed by, I blessed them and occasionally received a word of wisdom or knowledge for someone.

On the way back to my motel, we had to stop the car again for me.

Bonnie Argue offered to stay with me all night to be sure I was all right, but I assured her if she would leave her phone number in case of any emergency, I expected to be fine.

By morning the nausea had left. I only drank water, but the dizziness continued and I had to have assistance to walk.

Amid protests that I should stay at least one more day, or allow someone to accompany me to Denver, I wobbled my way in between two pairs of strong arms to board the plane.

I just refused to give any ground to Satan.

We weren't airborne for more than fifteen minutes when I was strongly impressed to read 1 Timothy 4:14-16 AMP:

> **Do not neglect the gift which is in you, [that special inward endowment] which was directly imparted to you [by the Holy Spirit] by prophetic utterance when the elders laid their hands upon you [at your ordination].**
>
> **Practice and cultivate and meditate upon these duties; throw yourself wholly into them [as your ministry], so that your progress may be evident to everybody.**
>
> **Look well to yourself [to your own personality] and to [your] teaching; persevere in these things [hold to**

them], for by so doing you will save both yourself and those who hear you.

Phillip had only been gone to heaven about three months, and I admit that I was hesitant to minister without him at my side, despite the wonderful, edifying and encouraging prophecies publicly and privately given to me by both Brother Hagin and Kenneth Copeland.

Now I was alerted!

I sat up straight in the plane seat and read that passage over and over.

Certainly I could remember when hands were laid on me at my ordination by the elders, one of whom was my own husband, Phillip; also Reverend Jim Kaseman, Reverend Mac Hammond and Dr. Frank Lindquist of the Assemblies of God, as well as others. I knew God was opening my eyes to my future ministry.

71

Phillip Goes Beyond the Veil

Although we had lived in St. Paul for over fifteen years and had a "For Sale by Owner" sign in our yard for three years, we hadn't had one offer.

Our son, who lived two miles away, had his phone number on one side of the sign, and our phone number was on the other side.

When we were in town from May 1 to November 1, we had the sign turned to show our number, and when we left for the winter to go to Dallas or Tulsa, we turned the sign again to show Jim's number.

No one had contacted us.

The reason we came back to Minnesota the last part of May 1985 was to look over an offer we had on the house. It was from a husband and wife, both doctors.

We met and talked with them about their offer.

"The offer is acceptable to us," said Phillip, "but we don't want to wait for you to sell your present house."

"That's no problem," said the man, "we can delete that part and change it to a cash offer." We were satisfied with that.

"Why don't you rewrite the purchase agreement," I suggested. "That way it will be neat and clean with no changes."

"We will do that and have it ready for you on June 11 when we meet at the mortgage company."

In the meantime, we went to Living Word Christian Center on Sunday morning, June 2. Roy Hicks was preaching.

Pastor Mac Hammond asked if we could be at the evening service as the church was about to launch its stewardship program and we were to help pray for that.

I remember so well in the morning service Pastor Hammond mentioning the stewardship program. Feeling so united with that church, I said to Phillip, "Let's be the first ones to give. How about writing the first check?"

Phillip got out his checkbook and wrote that check.

We were so happy. Even though we didn't have a church home because of ministering almost every Sunday and in between at different churches, we loved Pastor Mac and Lynne.

That Sunday evening Pastor Mac Hammond spoke of the future of the church and the urgency to enlarge. He asked Phillip to come up and pray with him.

What happened was quite unusual. Phillip almost jumped out of his seat and quickly walked up the steps to be with Pastor Mac. It was unusual because Phillip always took my arm and wanted me to be with him.

I automatically rose up from my chair, and since he had already gone ahead, I followed him.

Was there something he knew that no one else did? I think so.

Pastor Mac prayed, and then with great unction Phillip began to pray.

Suddenly, Pastor Mac and Phillip went down under the power of the Spirit.

Phillip landed face up, right at my knees. (I always knelt on the platform when Phillip prayed.)

As I was praying in the Spirit and looking down on my husband's face, he opened his eyes and looked at me. Then he closed his eyes for the last time, but I did not know it at that moment.

All efforts to revive Phillip proved fruitless. He slipped away while praying in the Spirit. How like him!

I rode with him in the ambulance to the hospital emergency room, where Lynne and I stayed with his body out of which his spirit had just ascended to heaven.

Brother Kenneth Hagin called me while I was in the hospital emergency room. "What a way to go!" he triumphantly spoke. "We should all be so fortunate!"

He spoke words of comfort to me and reminded me of Brother Gordon Lindsay, founder and pastor of Christ for the Nations. He left this earth while standing in the pulpit preaching. Yes, "what a way to go!"

Our son, Jim Halverson, is just like his father, tender and comforting. He and his wife, Kris, drove me to their home from the hospital.

I didn't sleep, but I sat upright in a lounge chair, just staring, as if in a cloud.

I felt so wrapped up, like in a cocoon—sheltered in my Father's embrace. None of us shed a tear.

The night before Phillip's celebration, we were at the mortuary to review the body and the casket and everything we'd picked out.

I knew Phillip wasn't there. He was in heaven, not in that casket.

The first thing I said was, "Where's his wedding ring? His wedding ring isn't here."

The man said, "Oh, I'll check into it," and he did, to no avail.

I said, "Well, check the hospital. Check the ambulance. He never took his wedding ring off. I just gave him a brand new one because the others we gave each other were worn out."

It seemingly could not be found.

The next morning the phone rang many times, but Jim and his wife took the calls at a distant phone. The living room was quiet. Jim and Kris came in, and we just looked at one another.

Suddenly, Jim left the room to return in a few minutes. I noticed his eyes were wet.

"Mom, God just spoke to me," he announced.

"Oh," I responded.

"God said He would speak to you in seven days." This was Monday, June 3.

All I could say was "Oh."

On Tuesday morning Brother Kenneth Copeland called. He spoke wonderful words of comfort to me and ended his conversation with, "We'll see you in two weeks at the Oklahoma City Convention."

I could not answer him. I could not imagine myself anywhere without Phillip.

After a long silence on my part, Brother Copeland continued, "The air ticket will be sent to you, as usual, and everyone is looking forward to your teaching."

Me? Teaching? Alone?

Finally, Brother Copeland said, "Fern, I'm not hanging up until you tell me you will be with us then. Say you will."

All I could say was "All right."

How could this be? People wanted to hear Phillip—not me. Everyone was in partnership with the ministry of the Holy Spirit through my *husband's* ministry—not mine.

But having been very honored with teaching in many of Kenneth Copeland's Conventions, I had confidence in his direction for me.

My pastor, Mac Hammond, and his wife, Lynne, spent time with Jim and me, not only in funeral arrangements, but also in loving comfort and words of cheer.

I never dreamed Phillip would precede me in going to heaven. I had talked to him several times about what he should be aware of in the event of my going to heaven—even though both of us looked forward to being "caught up forever to be with the Lord."

I had told Phillip that he would have to marry again. I did not want him to live alone.

Many calls and arrangements were made for Phillip's "celebration" on Thursday, June 6, at Living Word Christian Center.

I knew better than to ask Brother Kenneth Hagin to speak, as he had called me from meetings he was in, and I had heard him say that he never interrupted his meetings.

We were overwhelmed by food, flowers and cards.

I had been up the night before, writing down what I wanted for the order of the service and also planning for the graveside service.

I wanted Pastor Mac Hammond to be the speaker and allow a few minutes for other ministers who flew in for the celebration to share.

Brother Kenneth Hagin Jr. came and spoke too. Our meetings in his various conventions had been full of the spectacular.

Many ministers of the churches where Phillip and I had ministered came for the Wednesday evening service at the funeral home.

At Living Word on Thursday, Pastor Hammond gave the invitation for all present at Phillip's celebration to repeat the sinner's prayer.

Several people told me later of loved ones in attendance who witnessed to them of their decision to accept Christ as their personal Savior and Lord.

My elderly Aunt Ellen, who was very ill herself, attended. She had avoided the subject of "religion" all of her life.

She had testified to her only son that she had experienced forgiveness of sins at Phillip's celebration. Then she had died two weeks later.

Billye Brim blessed the graveside services, and I felt led to tell those assembled at the Fort Snelling Cemetery about an unusual experience I'd had the night before at the mortuary.

I told them that a week before we'd come back to Minneapolis to sell our house, I'd been wide awake at three o'clock in the morning. A fragment of Scripture had kept coming to my mind: **Of whom the whole family in heaven and earth....** I'd finally gotten up and looked for it in my Bible:

> **For this cause I bow my knees unto the Father of our Lord Jesus Christ, of whom the whole family in heaven and earth is named.**
>
> **Ephesians 3:14,15**

I began to realize the meaning of this Wednesday night at the mortuary.

In the days prior to Phillip's homegoing, off and on as Phillip had prayed in the Spirit, he'd kept saying the name "Trombley," along with other words. Phillip had speculated that he had worked with a Dr. Trombley.

The night of the celebration at the mortuary, as I was conversing with friends, a man approached me and introduced himself: "Mrs. Halverson, I'm Doc Trombley. Do you remember me?"

"Yes, I do remember you," I responded, being alerted by the Holy Spirit.

"I felt like I just had to come tonight," he said.

You see, the Spirit of God had already moved and he'd responded in the only way he could—*he had to be there!*

Taking his hand, I moved to a more distant place in this large room, where I pointed out the uncertainty of this life.

"Doc," I said, "you cannot be sure you will be able to put the key in your car as you leave here. You can't be sure you will even arrive home. You will live forever, Doc. Will it be heaven or hell?"

I am so happy to tell you that after a very brief, to-the-point conversation, I had the marvelous privilege of asking him if he would secure his salvation that very night by repeating a prayer with me.

He agreed to the freedom of forgiveness of sin! Hallelujah!

Phillip had prayed for this man a week earlier. Now, on the other side of the veil, he saw what the Spirit of God accomplished as a result of his prayers.

I wanted to contribute the money given to me as a memorial to Phillip to Living Word Christian Center. So the following Monday I presented Pastor Hammond with this addition to the stewardship fund.

On my way home, I decided to drive on Minnehaha Parkway by Lake Nokomis to reminisce the days of Phillip's and my courtship.

It was there, after seeing me off and on for a couple of months (he lived in another state), that he had first kissed me!

As I approached the area, something strange was happening. I felt good. It was a cool day, and all the car windows were shut.

Suddenly, I was aware that there were voices in the car. I pulled over to the curb.

"Beverly, Beverly, residence, permanent, Beverly residence, Beverly, Beverly...home...permanent."

I got the message: I was to make our home on Beverly Road my residence. I had planned to live in our home in Tulsa. I had no intention of moving back to St. Paul, as the house was empty.

It was so plain to me. I was to move back. I was on my way to my son's home, and I would tell Jim and Kris of my experience.

Jim and Kris listened intently. "Yes, Mom," Jim said, "that is what God told me last Monday. Remember, I told you God said He would speak to you in seven days?"

"Yes!"

"Today is the seventh day!"

I had a 3:30 appointment that day with the buyers of my house at their attorney's office. I was within two hours of completing the sale.

God had intervened at the eleventh hour to prevent me from selling!

The deposit money was refunded, and I had to make plans to move from Tulsa to St. Paul.

God had the whole scenario all set up. Plans were made for Jim to fly with me to Tulsa, leaving our Cadillac in St. Paul.

That first morning in my Tulsa home, I settled myself in the office to go through things.

"What can I do to help?" Jim offered.

I suggested he go through the office closet and dispose of odds and ends of luggage we had accumulated.

There were older ones, quite worn, and new ones, as well as a new set given to us that had never been used. (I gave it away to a ministry.)

The first item he emerged with was an attaché case we had used only a few times. He opened it and took out a zippered bank case. We used it for scissors, tape and so forth.

"Mom!" he cried. "Look!"

He held up Phillip's wedding ring—engraved and dated. It was the only item in the case!

It felt like electricity passed through me. I could hardly believe what I was seeing was Phillip's wedding ring. I held it and fondled it in an attempt to meld desire with the reality in my very hands.

Previously, while still in my St. Paul home, I had called North Memorial Hospital to tell them about Phillip's missing wedding ring.

They'd been very nice and instituted a search, which had resulted in a letter that suggested I'd let them know the price of the ring and they would pay me for it.

I did not want money. I wanted my wedding gift to Phillip!

I remember crying out loudly to the Lord and demanding, "God, I want that ring!"

When I told Billye Brim about it, she said, "An angel found it and brought it back to you!"

I believe that!

Jim flew back to Minneapolis, and I stayed in Tulsa, getting things sorted out for the move to St. Paul.

He shall give his angels charge over thee....

Luke 4:10

72

My New *Beginnings*

When I returned home perfectly well, the very first letter I opened from a stack of mail was from Vicki Jamison-Peterson.

When praying for me, she had been impressed to send me a check for printing and mailing expenses—a check for $2000!

I hadn't planned to mail anything. Thank-you notes kept me busy.

Just before the Santa Rosa trip, Marianna Bauer had come to me. "I want to be a help to you," she'd said.

All I could think of was occasional housework help.

"I can sew or mend, clean, type, duplicate tapes and many other things, so be sure to let me know how I can help you. I am impressed to offer my services to you," she had said so sweetly.

"Do you have any tapes you want duplicated?" she had inquired.

"No," I had replied. "All the churches and conventions we spoke at kept the master tapes, as we have no use for them."

Everywhere we had gone, people would inquire if they could obtain our tapes, but we had informed them that we didn't keep any and they could buy the meetings' tapes from the church or convention.

We'd never wanted to get into any kind of business with tapes.

A few days later, as I was unpacking more boxes from my move from Tulsa to St. Paul, I came across the huge, heavy box that had been delivered to us in Tulsa.

Phillip and I had come home from a two-week trip and picked up our mail. The next-door neighbor had delivered this large box to us that evening.

Curious, we'd immediately opened it to discover a state-of-the-art tape duplicator from Mac Hammond, of Living Word Christian Center, where we had ministered several times. We'd been dumbfounded.

Why would he send us a duplicator? We'd bought tapes to listen to, but we'd never duplicated any.

And the very next day Phillip had wanted to look up tape companies in Tulsa, so we'd arrived at a major tape distributor's office.

"What can I do for you?" the distributor had asked.

"We came to find out how tapes are bought and if you have some on hand," Phillip had said.

I had whispered to him that we *didn't need any tapes!*

Soon he and the distributor had been talking quantities and prices. I'd been so puzzled. I had *not* wanted to have any additional burden of tape duplicating. (I'd known Phillip would not do it!)

"Well," the distributor had said, "how many do you want to order?"

"Oh," Phillip had stated, "probably about six."

"Six!" the man had exclaimed. "I will just *give* you six."

I had been relieved, but then I'd heard Phillip say, "Show me your albums, please."

I'd interrupted to tell Phillip that we had several albums at home. "What do you want with some albums?" I'd asked. My question had gone unnoticed.

On the ride home I'd thought of these twelve four-place and six six-place albums that were on order for a two-week delivery.

In the meantime, Phillip had been promoted to his new job in heaven. Now here I was looking at a duplicator and a couple of unopened boxes of albums.

The unpacking from Tulsa was coming to a final finish! As I looked at the last box, I saw folders and manila envelopes to be sorted out in my office space.

Opening the last envelope labeled "Copeland," I reached in to bring forth a bunch of scraps of paper—each with a name or names with addresses of people who said, "If you ever put out any tapes, here is my name to notify."

That had gone on for several years, and I had just taken these papers, stuffed them into my purse and then put them into this envelope. I had forgotten all about them.

At the same time, our master tapes began arriving from different churches we had ministered at.

I called Marianna. "I need you!" I exclaimed excitedly.

"You will not guess what I have found!" I exclaimed. "Come over when you can, and be prepared for a surprise!" I announced.

Marianna went right to work that morning in my office, typing out the names and arranging them by different locations. There were 660 names!

After talking it over, I decided to go to the expense of sending these 660 people postcards announcing that I had some tapes and, if they were interested, they could contact me.

In a couple of weeks I had over 585 names and was ready to begin the process of obtaining a mailing permit, printing costs and so forth, for which Marianna took full charge.

She worked so diligently that when I would bring her a cup of coffee or whatever, she did not want to be interrupted.

Keeping track of the orders and organizing the mail grew to be a big job, and the mailings began to increase as more names were added from the meetings we were holding independently.

We never felt led to promote tapes, but we just wanted to let people know we had them. There was a phenomenal growth.

Add to that the book I have written, *Adventures with the Holy Spirit,* and a subsequent book, *Adventures with the Holy Spirit, Including the Scandinavian Story,* and you can imagine how busy Marianna was.

How grateful I am for her leading to help me. She became a full-time employee right away.

And to think Pastor Mac and Lynne Hammond, of Living Word Christian Center in Brooklyn Park (my church), had felt urged to send a tape duplicator way ahead of time!

Then Phillip had ordered the albums!

How like God to speak and confirm! He'd spoken to me on the plane about the words spoken to me at my ordination and by Brother Hagin and Kenneth Copeland.

The miracle of the tape ministry revealed God's plan.

Yes, I dragged my feet through most of it, but God saw my heart was fastened to Him, and He went ahead and did His plan. Selah!

> **A man's mind plans his way, but the Lord directs his steps and makes them sure.**
>
> **Proverbs 16:9** AMP

73

Moving *On!*

Ten years later, in the middle of October 1995, I decided to get my large home ready to sell instead of just talking about it.

Little by little, I sorted through twenty-six years of accumulation and blessed many people by giving much of it away.

Then I had an estate sale and disposed of more furniture and belongings.

I knew what I would like to buy in a new home, but viewing various condos and townhouses proved unproductive.

God impressed upon me that He had a residence for me and not to be concerned about it.

So I put it completely out of my mind. In fact, when friends suggested looking at various places, I knew immediately it was not for me. I was content to just get my home ready for sale.

I put a sign on the front lawn: "For Sale by Owner." Several couples viewed it but found objections.

I decided to call three realtors and choose one, which proved to be a wise move.

The one I chose lived only three blocks away, and she soon brought a prospective buyer through my home.

Then, my realtor called to tell me that a couple she had been showing over twenty houses to had "mistakenly" driven by my home and asked if they could view it.

This couple had actually decided on another home and were on their way to sign a contract when they'd taken a "wrong" turn and driven by my home!

They saw it on a Tuesday, and I had a purchase agreement that same evening. They wanted to move in the following Friday.

All of my papers had been verified ahead of time, and when I protested that I needed a couple more days at least to thoroughly clean it after moving, they said, "Don't bother. We are having an architect come in, and the first thing we will do is remove the carpeting and put in all wood floors."

Like a whirlwind, I had help from friends at church loading up the van and away I went to a temporary residence.

Later, I awakened in the middle of the night after having a dream about a place I had been in for a baby shower for a friend's daughter.

My dream was so real that I'd relived the pleasant experience. I seldom dream—and if I do, I rarely remember it. This was different. All that next day I thought about that house.

I remembered it had been for sale. In fact, my friend had been trying to get her daughter and husband to buy it. This had been at least three years earlier.

I could not put that house out of my mind, so finally I decided to call my friend who told me the owners had taken it off the market. She gave me the owners' phone number.

After another day, I called the couple, who said they were moving to Milwaukee and had recently talked about selling their house.

After arriving at a price and being able to assume their mortgage, which gave me a considerable savings, I purchased that house.

I believe God saved it for me!

The blessing of the Lord, it maketh rich, and he addeth no sorrow with it.

Proverbs 10:22

Godspeed!

As you embark on your journey with God, I wish you Godspeed. I wish you alive and active experiences in the Holy Spirit that will make these manifestations look like small incidents in the name of Jesus. Amen and amen.

Prayer of Salvation

Father, in the name of Jesus, I confess that I am unworthy of Your love and power. I have done nothing to deserve Your salvation, but Your Word says that Your grace and the blood of Your Son, Jesus Christ, give me the right to it. (1 Cor. 1:30; Phil. 3:9.)

So in the name of Jesus, I ask You to forgive me of my sins. I believe that Jesus is Your Son and that He died as a sacrifice for me. I believe that You raised Him from the dead and that, as my Advocate, He sits with You in the throne room of heaven.

Thank You for loving me so much that You gave Your Son for me and washed my sins away. I receive Him as my Savior and give You lordship of my life from this day forth, in Jesus' name. Amen.

Prayer for the Baptism in the Holy Spirit

Father, in the name of Jesus, I ask You to fill me with the Holy Spirit with the evidence of speaking in tongues. (Acts 2:4.)

Jesus, You said, **You shall receive power (ability, efficiency, and might) when the Holy Spirit has come upon you, and you shall be My witnesses...to the ends (the very bounds) of the earth.** I invite the Holy Spirit to come upon me so that I may be a witness of Your power in the earth today. (Now worship Him, expecting His power.)

Thank You, Lord, for filling me with Your Spirit, in the name of Jesus. Amen.

Endnotes

Chapter 10

[1] *The American College Dictionary* (New York: Random House, 1965), s.v. "santal."

Chapter 23

[1] *Merriam-Webster's Collegiate Dictionary,* 10th Ed., (Springfield, MA: Merriam-Webster, 1999), s.v. *inter-*.

[2] Ibid., s.v. *cession.*

References

The American College Dictionary. New York: Random House, 1965.

Holy Bible, New Living Translation. Wheaton, IL: Tyndale House, 1996.

Merriam-Webster's Collegiate Dictionary, 10th Ed. Springfield, MA: Merriam-Webster, 1999.

About the Author

Fern Halverson has been a teacher of the Old Testament for over fifteen years at Living Word Bible Institute, Brooklyn Park, Minnesota, as well as leading the weekly Bible and prayer class.

To contact Fern Halverson,

write or call

Living Word Christian Center

9201 75th Avenue North

Brooklyn Park, Minnesota 55428

(763) 315-7000

Please include your prayer requests

and comments when you write.

Other Books by
Phillip and Fern Halverson

Adventures With the Holy Spirit

Adventures With the Holy Spirit,
Including the Scandinavian Story

Available from your local bookstore.

Harrison House
Tulsa, Oklahoma 74153

The Harrison House Vision

Proclaiming the truth and the power

Of the Gospel of Jesus Christ

With excellence;

Challenging Christians to

Live victoriously,

Grow spiritually,

Know God intimately.